D1083307

THE TALMUD OF BABYLONIA
An American Translation
XXXV: Meilah and Tamid

Number 109
THE TALMUD OF BABYLONIA
An American Translation
XXXV: Meilah and Tamid

Translated by
Peter J. Haas

THE TALMUD OF BABYLONIA
An American Translation
XXXV: Meilah and Tamid

Translated by

Peter J. Haas

Scholars Press
Atlanta, Georgia

THE TALMUD OF BABYLONIA
An American Translation
XXXV : Meilah and Tamid

© 1986
Brown University

Library of Congress Cataloging in Publication Data

Talmud. Me'ilah. English
    Meilah and Tamid.

    (The Talmud of Babylonia; 35) (Brown Judaic
studies; no. 109)
    Includes index.
    I. Haas, Peter J. (Peter Jerome) II. Talmud.
Tamid. English. 1986. III. Title. IV. Series:
Talmud. English. 1984; 35. V. Series: Brown
Judaic studies; no. 109.
BM499.5.E4   1984 vol. 35   296.1'2505 s   86-26036
[BM506.M44E5]   [296.1'25]
ISBN 1-55540-086-8 (alk. paper)

Printed in the United States of America
on acid-free paper

In Memoriam

Milton Bendiner

זצ"ל

CONTENTS

This volume contains two tractates, Meilah and Tamid, for the new American translation of the Babylonian Talmud being published in the Brown Judaic Studies series. The reasons for this new translation, and the theories governing it, have already been explained amply by Jacob Neusner in his prefaces to Volumes I, VI, XVII, XXIII, and XXXII of the series. It suffices here simply to say that the purpose of this project is, first, to provide a translation specifically designed for the reader of American English, and, second, to present a translation that makes clear to the non-specialist the flow of the Talmud's argument. In distinction to earlier translations, then, this series aims primarily to convey to the reader the sense of the classical argument as it is developed through the form and content of its discourse.

At this point it may be helpful to point out some of the conventions that govern the presentation of this translation. To begin with, the translation presented here preserves the traditional organization of the Talmud by citing the relevant Mishnaic passage at the beginning of each block of the Talmud's discussion. The Talmud's discussion of this Mishnah-passage (the Gemara) is not presented as a single monolithic block, however, but is divided into what seem to me to be its constituent units of coherent discourse. These I have marked with Roman numerals. These larger units of discourse are themselves subdivided into their simplest elements. These elements, generally a sentence or a group of closely related sentences, have been labelled with capital letters. The reader thus encounters first the Mishnah-passage under consideration and then the large units of the Talmud's commentary, each itself presented so as to indicate its own formal structure. It is hoped that through this arrangement, the formal and topical construction of the entire discourse will become clear.

Because the translation is designed with the non-specialist in mind, it has been necessary to supplement the original Hebrew and Aramaic with at times considerable interpolated language. I have always placed this added language in brackets so that reader is aware of what appears in the original and what are my

comments.   References to Mishnah and Tosefta follow the notation standard
developed by Jacob Neusner and his students in their translations of these
Tannaitic texts.

It   remains for me to express my graditude to Prof. Joel Gereboff of Arizona
State University, who assiduously checked the entire manuscript against the
original text. I also owe a debt of gratitude to Prof. Alan Avery-Peck of Tulane
University, who read through the manuscript as it was being prepared for press
and whose many suggestions materially improved the translation.

Peter J. Haas
Nashville, TN
June 12, 1986
Sivan 5, 5746
Erev Shavuot

CHAPTER ONE

INTRODUCTION TO MEILAH

Meilah, translated here as sacrilege, occurs when an individual (unwittingly) takes for personal use an item that belongs to the holy altar. According to Scripture, one who commits such an act of sacrilege must repay the altar with an item worth 120% of the original (that is, the value of the misappropriated item plus a penalty of of an added one-fifth), in addition to bringing a guilt-offering. This much Mishnah and Talmud take for granted. At issue in the discussion before us is to determine the exact point at which an item designated for the altar becomes subject to meilah and at what time, if ever, it ceases to be so subject.

In these matters, Scripture is of little help. While Scripture provides the broad outline of the laws of sacrilege, it does not deal with the specifics of their application. The most detailed treatment of these laws in Scripture is Leviticus 5:15-16, which reads as follows:

> When a person commits a trespass (m'l), being unwittingly remiss about any of the Lord's sacred things, he shall bring as his penalty to the Lord a ram without blemish from the flock, convertible into payment in silver by the sanctuary weight, as a guilt-offering. He shall make restitution of that wherein he was remiss about the sacred things, and he shall add a fifth part to it and give it to the priest. The priest shall make expiation on his behalf with the ram of the guilt-offering, and he shall be forgiven. (JPS translation)

The problem for Mishnah's framers, as we said, is to determine at what point consecrated items enter the status of "the Lord's sacred things," and so become susceptable to sacrilege. Their theory is that items are "the Lord's sacred things" only when they are owed to the altar. The implication is that sacred items are exempt from sacrilege if they have not been properly prepared for the

altar or if the appropriate parts have already been given to the altar. The task
Mishnah's authorities set for themselves is to apply this theory to specific
sacrifices. In particular, they will work with the three categories of sacred
items they have already identified: Most Holy Things (animals designated to be
used as burnt-offerings or sin-offerings, for example), Lesser Holy Things
(peace-offerings, firstborn, thanksgiving-offerings) and items donated to the
Temple. Since each will be subject to sacrilege at different times in its
career, each is treated separately by the framers of Mishnah, and so by the
authorities of the Gemara as well. Let us now look briefly at the considerations
governing each of these.

We begin with animals destined for use as Most Holy Things. These become the
property of the altar as soon as they are designated for use as an offering.
Thus, according to Mishnah, they are subject to sacrilege from the very moment
they are separated from the herd or flock. They remain in this status until their
blood has been properly tossed and the appropriate meaty parts have been burnt on
the altar-fire. At this point the altar has been satisfied and the remaining
meat belongs to the priest. Mishnah regards this material as no longer subject
to the laws of sacrilege.

Similar considerations come into play for Lesser Holy Things. Beasts
designated for this purpose, however, are not deemed to be the property of the
altar until their blood has been correctly tossed. Consequently, for Mishnah's
framers, these animals do not become subject to the laws of sacrilege until that
time. That is, they only become subject to the laws of sacrilege after they are
given to the priest in Jerusalem, who slaughters them and sprinkles the blood
about the altar. Once this occurs, they become subject to sacrilege and then
remain susceptible until the requisite meat has been burnt on the altar,
satisfying the altar's claim. As before, once the altar is satisfied, the
remaining portions are no longer susceptible to further acts of sacrilege.

Items dedicated to the treasury for the upkeep of the Temple are Mishnah's
third category of holy things. Since these are dedicated specifically for the
altar, they become subject to sacrilege as soon as they are so designated and
remain in that status forever.

Working with these presuppositions, Mishnah, and then Talmud, investigate the details of when one is to apply the laws of sacrilege. The following outline of Mishnah's tractate reveals the topics of most concern to Mishnah's framers:

I. Sacrilege of sacrifices (1:1-3:8)

    A. When the laws of sacrilege apply (1:1-4)

        1:1 When the sacrifice belongs to the altar

        1:2-3 Meat of a Most Holy Thing goes forth beyond the veil—

            Eliezer: tossing the blood now has no effect and the meat

            remains subject to sacrilege. Aqiba: tossing the blood has

            effect.

        1:4   The effect of tossing the blood of Most Holy Things compared

            with tossing the blood of Lesser Holy Things.

    B. Stages in the Status of an Offering (2:1-9)

        2:1-5 At what point an animal becomes subject to sacrilege, may be

            invalidated by a Tebul Yom, is liable to the laws of refuse,

            remnant and uncleanness and becomes exempt from the laws of

            sacrilege.

        2:6-9 Meal- and incense-offerings.

    C. Cultic property which is not subject to the laws of sacrilege but
          which also is not to be used for non-cultic purposes (3:1-8)

        3:1-2 Items dedicated to the altar but which cannot be offered

        3:3   Blood, libations

        3:4-5 Ashes from the altar, bird-offerings that are too young or

            too old, milk and eggs from consecrated animals

        3:6   Items dedicated for theupkeep of the temple.

        3:7-8 Secular items connected to consecrated items

II. Sacrilege of Temple Property (4:1-6:6)

   A. Sacrilege occurs when a <u>perutah's</u> value is involved (4:1-6)

      4:1 Items dedicated to the altar or for the upkeep of the temple
         join together

      4:2 Five things in a burnt-offering join together

      4:3-6 All forms of refuse, remnant and carrion join together

   B. Sacrilege caused by a <u>perutah's</u> worth of benefit or damage. (5:1-2)

   C. Sacrilege causes the sacred item to become secular (5:3-5)

      5:3 Whether or not an item is subject to subsequent acts of
         sacrilege

      5:4 Sacrilege occurs when the item is actually used for secular
         purposes

      5:5 Separate acts of eating sacred food join together.

   D. Agency in affecting an act of sacrilege (6:1-5)

      6:1 An agent carrying out his commission is not responsible for
         sacrilege

      6:2 Minor agents are not responsible for sacrilege

      6:3 Any act of sacrilege must involve a <u>perutah's</u> value.

      6:4 The householder is not responsible for sacrilege of even two
         <u>perutah's</u> worth if his commission was not carried out.

      6:5 Money left with a money-changer

      6:6 Coins from a purse into which fell a consecrated coin.

Mishnah's discussion begins with sacrifices (Unit I). As we have seen, Most
Holy Things become subject to sacrilege as soon as they are designated for the
altar.   They become exempt again when their blood is tossed and the altar has
received its requisite share of the meat. At issue in this unit is the status of
the meat if the ritual preparation of the sacrifice is interrupted. Eliezer in
1:2 claims that the result is to invalidate all subsequent acts. Thus tossing
the blood of Most Holy Things will have no effect and the meat remains subject to
sacrilege forever. Conversely, the meat of Lesser Holy Things, which has not yet

become susceptible to sacrilege, now can never become so. Aqiba, holds the opposing view, namely that the tossing of the blood and other ritual acts continue to be efficacious, even though the meat is rendered unsuitable for the altar. Thus when the blood is tossed, Most Holy Things become exempt from sacrilege and Lesser Holy Things become suscepitble to sacrilege. Mishnah's framers have provided us, then, with a sustained and systematic inquiry into when various categories of sacrifices become susceptible to, or exempt from, sacrilege.

Unit II asks about items dedicated for the upkeep of the Temple. Since these are always subject to sacrilege, Mishnah's attention turns to defining precisely what constitutes misuse. A and B establish the minimum amount of deterioration that must be caused by secular use for sacrilege to occur. C then explores the notion that an item once appropriated for secular purposes becomes secular. If this is so, then the item is obviously immune from subsequent acts of sacrilege. D concludes by investigating how we assign responsibility for an act of sacrilege committed by an agent acting on someone else's behalf.

The Gemara, for its part, works closely with Mishnah's themes and concerns. For the most part Gemara's authorities are concerned with clarifying Mishnah's language and with providing Scriptural warrant for Mishnah's rulings. Only rarely will it initiate fresh topics for discussion.

The following translation is based on the Venice manuscript (designated "V") published in 1522 by Daniel Bomberg and reprinted by Maqor (Jerusalem, 1970). In those rare cases in which the standard printed edition differs, I indicate this with the siglum "B." Because of the Gemara's elliptical style, I have found it necessary to add considerable explanatory language. This is always set apart in square brackets. In adding explanatory language, I have regularly consulted the standard commentaries, as well as the translation of I. Porusch, Meilah. Translated into English with Notes and Indices (London: Soncino, 1948). Where I have found it helpful to cite Porusch verbatim, I have included this also in brackets. The Mishnah translations, as well as the outline above, are taken, with minor adjustments to preserve consistency of language, from J. Neusner, A History of the Mishnaic Law of Holy Things. Part Five (Leiden: Brill, 1980).

CHAPTER TWO

BAVLI MEILAH CHAPTER ONE

1:1

A. [2A] Most Holy Things which one slaughtered in the south [side of the altar]--

B. the laws of sacrilege apply to them.

C. [If] one slaughtered them in the south and received their blood in the north,

D. in the north and received their blood in the south,

E. [if] one slaughtered them by day and tossed the blood by night,

G. or [if] one slaughtered them [with the intention of eating that which is usually eaten or offering up that which is usually offered up] outside of their proper time or outside of their proper place-

H. the laws of sacrilege apply to them.

I. A general principle did R. Joshua state: "Whatever has had a moment of availability for [use by] the priests--the laws of sacrilege do not apply thereto.

J. "And [whatever] has not [yet] had a moment of availability to the priests-- the laws of sacrilege do apply thereto."

K. What is that which has had a moment of availability to the priests?

L. That which [after the proper tossing of the blood] has been left overnight, and that which has been made unclean, and that which has gone forth [beyond the veils].

M. And what is that which has not [yet] had a moment of availability to the priests?

N. That which has been slaughtered [with improper intention, e.g. to eat that which is usually eaten or to offer up that which is usually offered up], outside of its proper time or outside of its proper place,

O. and that, the blood of which invalid men have received, or tossed.

I.

A. [It has just been] taught on Tannaitic authority:

B. [As regards] most Holy things which one slaughtered on the south [side of the altar]--the laws of sacrilege apply [M.1:1A-B]:

C. This is obvious! [Why] should we exempt them from the laws of sacrilege just because one slaughtered them on the south [side of the altar instead of the north side]?

D. It is necessary [to state this because otherwise] you might have supposed that since R. Ulla said R. Yohanan said,   "Consecrated animals which die [without proper slaughtering] are exempt from the law of sacrilege by the very word of Torah," so most Holy things slaughtered on the south [side of the altar] which are like animals that were strangled [and not properly slaughtered, are also exempt from the laws of sacrilege].

E. Accordingly [Mishnah explicitly states that this is not the case].

F. [This answer to C is inadequate. While] consecrated animals that die are not suitable for the altar at all, animals slaughtered on the south side [of the altar], although not suitable for use as Most Holy Things, are [still] suitable for use as Lesser Holy Things. [Thus the situation envisioned by D is in all events impossible, and C's question remains unanswered.]

II.

A. Why [does the framer of this Mishnah passage] include all these cases [i.e., M.1:1 C-P] in his teaching?

B. It is necessary [for the following reason]: Had he taught only, If one slaughtered them in the south and received their blood in the north, [I might falsely conclude that] in this case the animal is subject to the laws of sacrilege only because [its blood] was properly received in the north; but if he had slaughtered it in the north and received its blood in the south -- since he recieved the blood [improperly] in the south, [the animal] becomes exempt from the laws of sacrilege.

C. [B. adds: Or had he taught only,] if he slaughtered them by day [and tossed the blood by night] [M:1:1E], I might falsely conclude [that in this case] the animal is subject to the laws of sacrilege only because the day is a

proper time for slaughtering, but if he slaughtered it by night and tossed
the blood by day -- since night is not the proper time for slaughtering, [the
animal] would be exempt from the laws of sacrilege.

D. [Or,] had he taught only, If he slaughtered it by night [and tossed the
blood by day] [M.1:F], I might falsely conclude [that in this case] the
animal is subject to the laws of sacrilege only because one received their
blood by day, but if he slaughtered it by day and tossed the blood by night -
-since night is not the proper time for slaughtering, [the animal] is like
one that was strangled and so is exempt from the laws of sacrilege.

E. Accordingly [M. includes all these cases to teach us that the laws of
sacrilege apply in either case].

III.

A. [If one slaughtered them with the intention of eating that which is usually
eaten or offering that which is usually offered up] outside of their proper
time or outside of their proper place [thereby invalidating them, they are
nonetheless subject to the laws of sacrilege] [M.1:1G]:

B. Of what use are [these animals such that they should still be subject to the
laws of sacrilege]?

C. [If their blood is properly received and tossed,] they enter the status of an
invalidated offering (piggul), [and so become consecrated, even though they
cannot be offered on the altar].

D. [2B] [The following question] was asked of them: If they bring [the offering
described in M.1:1G] up to the altar, must they take it down [or must they
leave it there]?

E. Rabbah said, "If they brought it up, they must take it down [since such an
offering is unfit for the altar]."

F. R. Joseph said, "If they bring it up, they do not take it down [because by
being placed on the altar the offering becomes like all other offerings, i.e.
the property of the altar]."

G. [Now, if Rabbah and Joseph agree] with the view of R. Judah [who holds that
any improper offering placed on the altar must be removed, Zeb. 84a], there

can be no [such] question [as D], for everyone would agree that if one brings
up to the altar [the invalidated offering described in M. 1:1G], they must
bring it down.

H. When can they disagree [such that D's question makes sense]? [Only] if
matters are in accord with R. Simeon [who holds that if invalidated animals
are placed on the altar they become the property of the altar and so must
remain].

I. [How do they disagree?] R. Joseph teaches in [apparent] strict accord with R.
Simeon [that any invalidated offering placed on the altar must remain
there].

J. Rabbah, [arguing that R. Simeon's view does not apply universally], says to
you, "R. Simeon is speaking only of the case in which the blood should have
been tossed on the upper part of the altar but was tossed on the lower part,
or should have been tossed on the lower part of the altar but was tossed on
the upper part, but in all events the priest slaughtered the animal and
received its blood [properly] in the north [side of the altar]. [In such a
case, Simeon says, the invalidated offerings is still consecrated and so must
remain on the altar.]

K. But here [concerning the offering of M. 1:1G], since the priest [wrongly]
slaughtered [the animal] in the south [side of the altar], it is like an
animal that was strangled [and so does not belong to the altar at all. If
this offering is taken up to the altar, even Simeon would agree that it must
be taken down. We thus see that D-F make sense only in the context of
Simeon's opinion.]"

IV.

A. [We shall now try to determine which interpretation of Simeons's view, that
of Rabbah or that of Joseph, is correct.] We have learned on Tannaitic
authority:

B. Most Holy Things which one slaughtered in the south [side of the altar]--the
laws of sacrilege apply [M. 1:1A-B]:

C. This seems certainly to be in agreement with R. Joseph [who holds in III.F
that invalid offerings placed on the altar must remain there].

D. But it is a problem as regards Rabbah [who holds in III.E that if such offerings are placed on the altar, they must be taken down. If this is so, they should also be exempt from the laws of sacrilege.]

E. [Mishnah's ruling is not really a problem for Rabbah.] Why [does Mishnah say that] the laws of sacrilege apply? [It says so only] because of a rabbinic enactment. [But according to Scripture the laws of sacrilege do not apply, in line with Rabbah's rule.]

F. What practical difference does it make whether the law is based on Scripture or on a rabbinical decree?

G. [The difference is in the amount he must pay if he misuses the animal. If its use is prohibited] by Scripture, he must pay [back its full value plus] an added fifth (Lev. 5:16). [If its use is prohibited] by rabbinic decree [he pays back only the animal's value], but not [the added fifth].

H. [But] is it indeed the case that the laws of sacrilege applies here only by rabbinic decree [and not according to Scripture]?

I. Yes! [We see this is so from] what Ulla said R. Yohanan said, "If Holy Things die, the laws of sacrilege no longer apply [according to the] word of Scripture."

J. [Ulla and Yohanan specify that this is "according to Scripture" to inform us that] according to Scripture the laws of sacrilege do not apply, but according to the rabbis they do apply.

K. Likewise here, [the laws of sacrilege do not apply according to Scripture, but the laws of sacrilege do apply] according to the rabbis.

L. [I-K seem unnecessary, for] one may say, "I have already learned what Ulla said R. Yohanan said [from our Mishnah-passage, which states explicitly that Holy Things slaughtered in the wrong place are subject to the laws of sacrilege]."

M. Even though I already learned this, it is necessary to state Ulla's [teaching here].

N. [For were it not stated here], you might suppose that I am saying [that only when the animal is slaughtered in the south side of the altar do we apply the laws of sacrilege because otherwise] people will not hesitate to touch it [and will thereby become unclean].

O. But as regards Holy Things which die, since people will surely avoid touching them, we do not apply the laws of sacrilege even by rabbinic decree.

P. Accordingly [we cite Ulla's teaching to show that the laws of sacrilege apply also in the case of those that died].

Q. [Further, I-K are necessary for the following reason:] As regards [Holy Things] that died I have also learned, "If one derives benefit from a living animal set aside as a sin-offering, this one does not commit sacrilege unless he causes the animal to become blemished; but if the animal is dead, he commits sacrilege as soon as he derives any benefit from it at all."

R. [Were it not for I-K,] you might suppose [3A] that I am saying [that we apply the laws of sacrilege] only if the animal is being brought as an atonement-offering, for otherwise people will not avoid touching it [and will thereby become unclean].

S. But as regards Holy Things, since these are not being brought as an atonement, people will in all events avoid touching them, and so we do not need to apply the laws of sacrilege.

T. Accordingly [we need Ulla's teaching to show that the laws of sacrilege apply in either cases].

U. [An objection is raised:] Is it indeed the case that the laws of sacrilege apply to an animal which was designated as a sin-offering and which then died [as Q claims]?

V. Have we not learned, "[As regards] animals designated as sin-offerings which [are left to] die and [consecrated] money [which must be cast into] the Dead Sea—one may not derive benefit from them, but the laws of sacrilege do not apply"?

W. They respond [as follows], "As for animals designated as sin-offerings which [are left to] die—people avoid touching them even while they are alive, [so applying the laws of sacrilege to these is unnecessary].

X. "This excludes animals designated as sin-offerings which are being kept alive [for the altar, however], for people do not hesitate to touch these. [In order to keep people from touching these, we must state explicitly that if the animal dies, the laws of sacrilege apply, as Q has said.]"

V.

A. R. Joseph, [who holds that invalid offerings must remain on the altar, IIIF]
   refuted the view of Rabbah, [who holds that they must be removed, IIIE] by
   reading [three Mishnah passages] in light of each other.

B. [The first is:] None of these [items listed in M. Zeb. 7:1-2] impart
   uncleanness to the garments of the one who swallowed [them], and the laws of
   sacrilege apply to them--except for the sin-offering of the fowl which one
   prepared below [the mid-point of the altar, that is,] in accord with the
   [proper rules for preparing] a sin-offering which is used as a sin-offering
   [M. Zeb. 7:3].

C. [In conjunction with this] he read [the following Mishnah-passage]: Any
   sacrificial [bird] which becomes invalid [while] in the Sanctuary does not
   impart uncleanness to the garments of the one who swallows [it]; but if it
   did not become invalid [while] in the Sanctuary [i.e., it became invalid
   elsewhere] it does impart uncleanness to the garments of the one who swallows
   [it = M. Zeb. 7:5L-M].

D. [In conjunction with this] he read [this third Mishnah-passage]: Anything,
   the invalidity of which [occurred] in the Sanctuary--if they placed it on the
   altar, they may not take it down [M. Zeb. 7:2D].

E. [From these passages, R. Joesph argues as follows: B tells us that the laws
   of sacrilege can apply to certain invalid sacrifices. C says this is so if
   the sacrifice was rendered invalid while in the Sanctuary. D then states
   that all items rendered invalid while in the Sanctuary belong to the altar.
   It follows that if this invalid offering is placed on the altar, it must
   remain there.] Is this not an [effective] refutation of Rabbah? [Indeed it
   is an effective] refutation!

F. The issue about which Rabbah and R. Joseph disagree [namely, whether or not
   invalid offerings belong to the altar] is [apparently] obvious to R. Eleazar
   [their predeccesor], for R. Eleazar says, "An offering designated for a
   personal altar but which one has brought into the Sanctuary [3B] becomes the
   property of the Holy Precinct in all respects [even though it is invalid].
   [This late Tannaitic master, then, seems to take an unequivocal stand on an
   issue later debated by Amoraic authoities.]"

G. [As we shall now see, however, Eleazar did in fact raise an issue related to
that of Rabbah and Joseph:] Yet R. Eleazar goes on to ask, "With regard to an
offering designated for a private altar [i.e. one of the ancient holy places
outside Jerusalem, such as Jacob's altar at Beth El] and which one then
brought into the [Jerusalem] Sanctuary [and which then] become invalidated:
if they brought it up to the altar, must they bring it down?"

H. Should we assume that he asks only about this particular case because [the
law as regards all other cases] is obvious to him--either as being in
accordance with Rabbah or as being in accordance with R. Joseph?

I. No, [on the contrary, R. Eleazar] asks about this one case in order [to
determine how to resolve] the case, [for as matters now stand he can resolve
this question either according to Rabbah or according to Joseph. And thus he
does not rule unequivocally as F implies.]

J. [He can reason like Rabbah] for did not Rabbah say, "If the offerings are
taken up [to the altar], they must be taken down"? [This is so only if the
offerings] were properly [assigned] to the Holy Precinct but were invalidated
[by being slaughtered on the south side of the altar]. But if the offerings
were not properly [assigned] to the Holy Precinct [to begin with], they
cannot become invalid [and so must remain on the altar].

K. On the other hand, [he can reason] like R. Joseph, who said, "If they are
taken up to the altar, they may not be taken down." [This is so only] if
they were properly [assigned] to the Holy Precinct and so became its
property. But if they were not properly [assigned] to the Holy Precinct,
they do not become its property [and so must be taken down].

L. [There is no way for Eleazar to determine which logic is more appropriate and
so the question] stands [unresolved].

VI.

A. Said R. Giddal said Rab, "Tossing the blood of a disqualified offering [has
no effect. It] does not exempt Most Holy Things from the laws of sacrilege,
nor does it cause Lesser Holy Things to become subject to the laws of
sacrilege."

B. Abayye was sitting and relating this teaching. R. Papa challenged Abayye, "[To the contrary, disqualified offerings can have an effect. True, if] one slaughters a thank-offering, [a Lesser Holy Thing,] inside the Holy Precinct while the bread [to be offered with it] is outside the Holy Precinct, he has not made the bread holy. Or if he slaughtered it [while the bread is still being baked] in the oven and has not yet formed a crust, or while all [of the loaves] except for one formed a crust, he has not made the bread holy. [But if the bread is ready and] he slaughtered [the thank-offering] outside of its proper time or outside of its proper place, he does render the bread holy. Consequently, [we see that] a disqualified offering does have effect [in so far as] it causes the bread to become subject to the laws of sacrilege."

C. [Abayye] was silent [i.e., he could not respond].

D. When [Abayye] came [and reported this conversation] to R. Abba, [R. Abba] said to him, "[You could have easily answered R. Papa, for his argument does not address the issue at hand, namely, what the effect of] tossing [the blood is]."

E. Said R. Ashi to Raba, "[I can prove that tossing the blood of a disqualified offering has effect in that it exempts Most Holy Things from the laws of sacrilege,]

F. "for does not Ulla say, 'If the handful of meal [to be placed on the altar] is disqualified but is [nonetheless] placed on the altar, its status of disqualification disappears [Zeb. 43a]'?

G. "Now taking the handful of meal is equivalent to slaughtering the animal, [and placing the meal on the altar is equivalent to tossing the animal's blood on the altar. It follows that just as placing a disqualified meal-offering on the altar renders it subject to the laws of sacrilege, so likewise does tossing the blood of a disqualified sacrifice render it subject to the laws of sacrilege. This refutes Giddal in A who said that tossing the blood of a disqualified offering has no effect whatsoever.]

H. [Raba] responds [to Ashi, "This is not proof, for the meal-offering in question is not really disqualified. Ulla is merely saying that if one takes

the meal-offering <u>intending</u> to use it] improperly in a way that would
disqualify it [but <u>in fact</u> places it on the altar correctly, it does not
become disqualified]."

I.   [4A] [Ashi replies to Raba, "Your interpretation of Ulla is wrong,] for since
he teaches that improper intention disqualifies other parts of the sacrifice,
it certainly follows that [improper intention] will disqualify [the meal-
offering]. So here, too, we have an act that renders the meal-offering
actually disqualified [as the analogy drawn in G requires]."

J.   Said Rabina to R. Ashi, "[Let us approach the issue from another angle:]
Does not Ilpa say, 'The dispute [between sages and Judah regarding the status
of an offering that was unacceptable both as disqualified (<u>piggul</u>) and as
unfit (<u>pasul</u>)] assumes two separate acts: for example [if the priest] says,
'Lo, I shall sever the windpipe [while purposing to use it] outside its
proper time (= <u>piggul</u>), and I shall sever the gullet [while purposing to use
it] outside its proper place (= <u>pasul</u>)'"? [According to Ilpa's proposal, we
can understand Judah to hold that the second act is of no consequence, since
it was done to an animal already disqualified as <u>piggul</u> by improper intention
(Giddal's view), while sages assume that both acts have effect (Ulla).]
[Ilpa goes on to say,] 'But if [both improper intentions concern the same
act], then everyone can agree that this is a mixed intention [and that the
animal is therefore neither fully disqualified as <u>piggul</u> nor fully unfit as
<u>pasul</u>, Cf Zeb 29B].'

K.   "If [Ilpa] is correct, then let the act of tossing the blood reveal whether
[the priest] had [both] improper intentions regarding one act [i.e., the
slaughtering] or two acts [i.e., the slaughtering and the tossing]." [For if
the priest had a distinct improper intention as regards each individual act,
that is, if he intended to eat the animal outside its proper time while
slaughtering, and then purposed to eat it outside its proper place when
tossing the blood, then the carcass would be <u>piggul</u>, as a result of his first
improper intention. If, on the other hand, both improper intentions applied
to the same single act, then the carcass would be both <u>piggul</u> and <u>pasul</u> at
the same time.]

L. [Ashi rejects Ilpa's view on the grounds that] if it were so, [we should be
    unable to establish the status of the meal-offering brought with the] thank-
    offering until its blood were tossed. [Yet we can establish its status
    before the blood is tossed—cf. B. Ilpa's view that two improper intentions
    can sometimes attach to a single act must therefore be wrong.]

VII.

A. [Reverting to R. Papa's statement in VI.B:] What [does he mean by saying
    that the bread becomes] holy?

B. [He means that it enters the status of] a disqualified offering and must be
    burned.

VIII.

A. May we say that the following supports [R. Giddal's view that tossing the
    blood of a disqualified offering has no effect]: "A disqualified offering is
    forever subject to the law of sacrilege"? Does this not mean that even if
    the blood is tossed [the animal remains in its prior status]?

B. Does this in fact support [R. Giddal]? No. [It assumes] that one has not
    yet tossed the blood, [so that of course the animal is still subject to the
    laws of sacrilege. It is only after one has tossed the blood, that the
    animal would be exempt from the laws of sacrilege.]

C. [The argument in B is unacceptable,] for if one has not tossed the blood, why
    say anything? [Everyone knows that before the blood is tossed, Most Holy
    Things remain subject to the laws of sacrilege. Thus the teaching in A must
    mean that the offering remains subject to sacrilege] even after one tossed
    the blood.

D. [Yet even on this reading, A still does not support Giddal's view] for it
    may refer only to burnt-offerings [which remain subject to sacrilege in all
    events until they are fully burnt. All other offerings, however, do become
    exempt from the laws of sacrilege upon the tossing of the blood.]

E. [This reading of A is now also shown to be unacceptable: A cannot refer only
    to] burnt-offerings, for this would be obvious since a burnt-offering is
    entirely God's [and so subject to sacrilege until it is fully burnt. Thus A
    must be referring to all offerings.]

F. [4B] And [here is yet] another way [to prove D wrong]: for the second half of
the teaching says, "If he left the blood overnight, even if he goes back and
tosses it [the next day, the animal] remains subject to the laws of
sacrilege." [This proves D wrong for] this makes sense only if you claim
that [A] refers [to both burnt-offerings] and sin-offerings [since their
blood must be properly tossed to make them fit for the priests]. But if you
say [A] refers only to a burnt-offering [--as D does--], can this be said!
[Such a statement would be nonsense, since properly tossing the blood of a
burnt-offering has no effect as regards the laws of sacrilege. This proves
that A cannot refer to burnt offerings alone, but must also refer at least to
sin-offerings.]

G. This last clause [cited in F] certainly supports [R. Giddal]. But does the
first clause [cited in A support him, as well]?

H. [Yes,] since the second clause supports [R. Giddal], the first clause also
must support him.

I. Does the second clause [cited in F] in fact support him, however?

J. For what difference should it make [if he left blood overnight (F), or if he
intended to leave part of the sacrifice overnight, thus disqualifying it (A)?
In either case the animal remains subject to the laws of sacrilege. So the
rule cited in F adds nothing new to the rule cited in A.]

K. [The difference is that] if he left the blood overnight, which is a physical
act, then his subsequent tossing of the blood [has no effect] and does not
exempt the offering from the laws of sacrilege; but if he only intended to
leave it overnight, which is not a physical act, then [the act of] tossing
the blood [overrides the intention and has effect, i.e.,] it exempts the
offering from the laws of sacrilege. [So F does add a new thought distinct
from A.]

L. May we say that [the following] supports [R. Giddal]: "A disqualified Most
Holy Thing is subject to the laws of sacrilege"? Does this not mean even if
the blood is tossed [that is, that tossing the blood has no effect]?

M. Does this support him? No! [It assumes that] he has not tossed the blood,
[so of course the animal is still subject to the laws of sacrilege].

N. But what is the law after he tossed the blood?

O. Now it too is not subject to the law of sacrilege. [That is tossing the blood has effect.]

P. [The followers of R. Giddal invoke the following to prove that tossing the blood has no effect:] "Why does the second clause [of the teaching in L] say, '[A disqualified] Lesser Holy Thing is not subject to the laws of sacrilege'? [It says this to show that in all events the status of a disqualified offering does not change when the blood is tossed. If it were otherwise,] let him make a distinction in the opening clause and say, 'Before he tosses the blood the Most Holy Thing is subject to the laws of sacrilege; after he tosses the blood it is no longer subject to the laws of sacrilege.' [Since he does not say this, we conclude that tossing the blood has no effect.]"

Q. This teaching certainly supports [R. Giddal].

R. Now can we say that since the second clause supports R. Giddal, the first one [= L] does also?

S. No! [The two clauses deal with different matters.] For as regards [disqualified] Lesser Holy Things [= P], the law is clear [that tossing the blood has no effect]. But as regards this case [i.e. disqualified Most Holy Things, L], the law is not yet clear.

IX.

A. A general principle did Joshua state: "Whatever has had a moment of availability to the priests--the laws of sacrilege do not apply thereto. And [whatever] has not [yet] had a moment of availability to the priests--the laws of sacrilege do apply thereto." What is that which has had a moment of availability to the priests? That which [after the proper receiving of the blood] has been left overnight, and that which has been made unclean, and that which has gone forth [beyond the veil]. And what is that which has not [yet] had a moment of availability to the priests? That which has been slaughtered [with improper intention to eat that which is usually eaten or to offer up that which is usually offered up] outside of its proper time or outside of its proper place, and that, the blood of which invalid men have received or tossed [M. 1:1/I-O]:

B. Said Bar Kappara to Bar Pada (B.: Pedat), "Son of my sister, note this which you are to ask me tomorrow in the study session: 'Do we teach that [holy things become] permitted [to the priest] when [properly] slaughtered [5A] or do we teach that [they become] permitted when [they are ready for the] tossing [of the blood] or do we teach that [they become] permitted when [they are ready for] eating?'"

C. Hezekiah said, "We teach that [holy things become] permitted [to the priest] when [properly] slaughtered."

D. R. Yohanan said, "We teach that [they become permitted] when [they are ready for] eating."

E. Said R. Zera, "Our Mishnah-passage is not specific [enough] to decide in favor of either] Hezekiah or R. Yohanan."

F. [The following argues that holy things become available to the priest when they are ready for the blood to be tossed.] We learned in our Mishnah-passage: [What is that which has had a moment of availability to the priests?] That which [after the proper receiving of the blood] has been left overnight, and that which has been made unclean, and that which has gone forth beyond the veil]. Does this not mean that it is the blood [that has been left overnight]? And it teaches [further] that the laws of sacrilege do not apply [in this case].

G. Consequently, we conclude that [holy things become] permitted [to the priest, such that the laws of sacrilege cease to apply, as soon as the blood is properly received and so is ready] to be tossed.

H. [The following argues that holy things become permitted to the priests when ready to be eaten, as Yohanan maintains in D:] No! [The Mishnah-passage assumes] that it is the meat that was left overnight after the blood was properly tossed. It is for this reason that we say the laws of sacrilege do not apply [namely, because the blood had been tossed, rendering the meat ready to be eaten].

I. [The following argues F's point that the crucial time is when the blood is ready to be tossed:] We learn in the Mishnah-passage: And what is it that has not [yet] had a moment of availability to the priest? That which has

been slaughtered [with improper intention to eat that which is usually eaten
or to offer up that which is usually offered up] outside of its proper time
or outside of its proper place, and that, the blood of which invalid men have
received or tossed.

J. How are we to understand this [last clause]? Am I to assume that it means
   that we must have invalid [priests both] receiving the blood and tossing it?
   But why must we have two [improper acts to render the offering unfit]? Does
   it not mean rather [that the offering is disqualified either when an invalid
   priest receives the blood or when an invalid [B.: valid] priest tosses it?
   [RASHI, reading with B, explains the passage as follows: Does it not mean
   rather that if invalid priests received the blood, that the laws of sacrilege
   apply even though it was then tossed by valid priests?" In either case, the
   point is the same, namely that if only one of the acts is performed by
   invalid priests, then the offering is made unfit.]

K. Now we teach in the Mishnah-passage [regarding this offering] that the laws
   of sacrilege apply. [This must be so because the blood was improperly
   received. It follows that if the blood had been properly received, the laws
   of sacrilege would cease to apply.] Thus we see [that the laws of sacrilege
   cease to apply when the blood is properly received and so ready] to be
   tossed.

L. R. Joseph answered him, "Do you think [the Mishnah-passage means] to treat
   separately [improper receiving and improper tossing? In fact, Mishnah means
   that both acts are to be considered together.]

M. "For we are taught [in Zeb. 92a]: 'As for an invalid sin-offering, its blood
   does not need to be washed off [of a garment on which it splattered] whether
   it had a moment of availability before it was rendered invalid or whether it
   did not have a moment of availability before it was rendered invalid.'"

N. What is that which has had a moment of availability and then was rendered
   invalid? That, the blood of which was left overnight, or which was rendered
   unclean or which went forth beyond the veil [=M. 1:1L].

O. What is that which did not have a moment of availability before it was
   rendered invalid? That which has been slaughtered [with the improper

intention of eating its meat] outside of its proper place or outside its
proper time and that the blood of which an invalid priest received and tossed
[=M. 1:1N]. [Receiving and tossing are here considered together.]

P. How is this to be understood? Might we say that when invalid priests both
received the blood and tossed the blood, then the blood need not be laundered
off; but when valid priests [both] received and tossed the blood, it does
need to be laundered off. [In either case the receiving and the tossing are
considered together, as Joseph says in L.]

Q. [The following proves to the contrary that receiving the blood and tossing
the blood are to be regarded separately:] Read [Lev. 6:20 as follows:
"When] any of the [received] blood will be tossed [on a garment, you shall
wash it. . .]" -- i.e., you need not wait until the blood has already been
tossed. [That is, if the blood has been properly received, but is yet to be
tossed, we consider the offering to be valid on the basis of the reception of
the blood alone.]

R. [Since we have now shown that on the basis of Scripture that receiving the
blood and tossing the blood are to be regarded separately, we must conclude
that the wording of the relevant ruling in M. Zeb. 10:1, which seems to
imply the opposite,] is inexact. [5B] It then follows that the statement of
the law here [in M. 1:1N] is also inexact. [P's interpretation of Mishnah is
thus to be rejected.]

S. Said R. Assi, "If [what you say about Mishnah's language being inexact] is
true, why do I find this phrase used twice [i.e. in M. Zeb 10:1 and here in
M.1:1N]?

T. "Rather, we must assume that [Mishnah] always use precise [language] as
regards the laws of sacrilege. [We therefore must interpret the future tense
in Leviticus 6:20 differently. I say it uses future tense to] teach us that
when an unfit [person tosses the blood, he] turns [any remaining blood into
an unfit] remnant [which may not be tossed in the future to render the meat
fit for the priests]. Thus even if an invalid person received [the blood]
and tossed it, and then a valid person received [a second portion of blood]
and tossed it, this [second tossing] amounts to nothing. What is the

reason? The blood is [now deemed to be an unfit] remnant. [In this way we can interpret Scripture such that it does not force us to abandon the clear meaning of Mishnah's rulings.]"

U. But lo, Resh Laqish asked R. Yohanan, "[Is it in fact true, as Assi says, that if] an invalid priest [tosses some of the blood the rest is] an unfit remnant?"

V. And he said to him, "[No.] The only way to make the remaining blood [unfit as] remnant is [to toss the blood with the improper intention of eating the meat] outside its proper time or outside its proper place, since [only the act of tossing the blood has the power] to disqualify offerings [not the status of the priest]."

W. [But] is this not the case also if [the blood is tossed] by an invalid priest, [namely that the remaing blood is not unfit as remnant]?

X. No! [W holds] even [if an invalid priest tosses the blood], for [W's statement says explicitly]: "The only way. . ." [thus excluding unvalidation by an unfit priest].

Y. This is what [W] means to say: The only act which does not render a public sacrifice acceptable and yet renders the blood [unfit as] remnant is [tossing the blood with the improper intention of] eating its meat outside its proper time or outside its proper place.

Z. That is, an unclean priest may offer a valid public offering and [with improper intention] can render [the blood unfit as] remnant. But priests rendered invalid for other reasons, who may not offer public-offerings, cannot render [blood unfit as] remnant.

X..

A. [We revert to the previous discussion as regards when the laws of sacrilege cease to apply.] Come and hear: "A disqualified [Most Holy Thing] is forever subject to the laws of sacrilege [= VIII.A]":

B. [Does this teaching not mean that disqualified Most Holy Thing remains subject to sacrilege] only because [the priest] is not yet ready to toss [the blood]?

C. Consequently, we learn [from A] that the laws of sacrilege cease to apply [even to a disqualified offering] when the blood is ready to be tossed.

D. No, [this interpretation is incorrect. A assumes that the priest is ready]
to toss the blood. What is the meaning of the word "forever"? It means that
the law is in accord with R. Giddal [who holds that if an offering is
disqualified, no further act on its behalf has effect and so it remains
subject to sacrilege forever].

E. For R. Giddal said [in the name] of Rab, "Tossing the blood of a disqualified
offering [has no effect. It] does not exempt [Most Holy Things] from the law
of sacrilege, nor does it cause [Lesser Holy Things] to become subject to the
law of sacrilege" [= VI/A].

F. [6A] Come and hear: R. Simeon says, "[If we were to say that offerings
become exempt from sacrilege when the blood is ready to be tossed, in accord
with A, then] there would be leftovers [i.e., meat not eaten by sunset] which
are subject to the laws of sacrilege, and leftovers which are not subject to
the laws of sacrilege [T. 1:3].

G. "How so? If [the meat] were left overnight before the blood was ready to be]
tossed, it would be subject to the laws of sacrilege [since it was never
rendered exempt. If it was left overnight] after the blood was ready to be]
tossed, it would not be subject to the laws of sacrilege [because the
prepared blood renders it exempt. Simeon's point is that such a conclusion
is absurd, so that B-C's interpretation of A must be wrong.]

H. "[The proper rendering of the law is as follows:] Now it is taught that
[sacrificial meat left overnight before the blood is tossed] is subject to
the laws of sacrilege. Was there not in fact time in this case actually to
toss the blood so that had he wanted to he could have tossed it? [Surely
there was. Then why did he not toss it? Because there was no time in any
case to eat it before sunset.]

I. "On the basis of this reasoning our conclusion must be that holy things are
exempt [from the laws of sacrilege not when the blood is ready to be tossed
but only] when [the meat is ready] to be eaten."

J. [We now argue that in fact B-C's interpretation of A is correct: Simeon's
fallacy lies in the fact that the ruling in H assumes that the blood was]
received just before sunset such that there really was no time to toss it

[before sundown. Its proper interpretation, then, is that the meat is exempt from the law of sacrilege when the blood is ready to be tossed.]

K. But what if there had been time [to toss the blood before sunset but the priest simply chose not to]? [In this case] likewise the meat would be exempt from the laws of sacrilege [because we regard blood ready to be tossed as though it were tossed].

L. [This last statement contradicts Mishnah's language. If blood ready to be tossed is regarded as though it were tossed,] what is the point of saying explicitly "before the blood is tossed"? Let it say "before sunset [while there is time to toss the blood]," or "after sunset" [when the collected blood no longer can be tossed].

M. In fact Mishnah's language conveys this same sense. ["Before the blood is tossed" means] before it is ready to be tossed; ["after the blood is tossed" means] after it is ready to be tossed.

XI.

A. Come and hear: R. Simeon says, "There is a kind of disqualified offering that is subject to the laws of sacrilege, and there is a kind of disqualified offering that is not subject to the laws of sacrilege.

B. "How so? Before [its blood] is tossed, it is subject to the law of sacrilege; after [its blood] is tossed, it is not subject to the law of sacrilege." [That is, Simeon is arguing again that tossing the blood of a disqualified offering has effect.]

C. But [this stands in contradiction to] a Tannaitic authority who has taught: "[If an offering is disqualified] before its blood is tossed, it remains subject to the laws of sacrilege [forever, even after the blood is tossed, Cf. VIII. A]."

D. [Simeon can respond:] Is this not so when there was time [before sunset] for him to toss [the blood] had he wanted to [but the priest chose not to]? [In this case] the offering remains subject to the laws of sacrilege [simply because the blood was not tossed. From this I conclude that [the laws of sacrilege] cease to apply [only after the blood is tossed and the meat is ready] to be eaten [Cf X. I].

E. [The following refutes D:] No, [the aforementioned ruling assumes there] was
   no time to toss [the blood before sunset and that is why the laws of
   sacrilege continue to apply].   But had there been time to toss the blood
   [what would the case be? We would have regarded the blood as though it were
   tossed and as such it would] exempt the sacrifice from the laws of sacrilege.
   [So the laws of sacrilege cease to apply when the blood is ready to be
   tossed.]

F. If so, why does [C explicitly] teach, "after tossing [the blood]"? Rather,
   let it say, "before sunset [i.e., available to be tossed]" or "after sunset
   [i.e., not available to be tossed."   Since it does not say this, I conclude
   that the laws of sacrilege cease to apply only when the blood is actually
   tossed, not when it is merely ready to be tossed.]

G. Similarly, [if the offering were rendered exempt from the laws of sacrilege
   when the blood was merely ready to be tossed], let Mishnah teach, "before the
   blood is fit to be tossed" or "after the blood is fit to be tossed." [Since
   Mishnah does not so specify, we must conclude that the offering is exempt
   from the laws of sacrilege only when the blood is actually tossed.]

H. [We now offer yet another proof that disqualified offerings are exempted from
   the laws of sacrilege only when their blood is actually tossed.]   Come and
   hear: "Disqualified [Most Holy Things] are subject to the laws of
   sacrilege."

I. Does this not assume [that we are talking about a time after] the blood was
   tossed? [Otherwise this ruling would be superfluous since before the blood
   is tossed the animal is of course subject to the laws of sacrilege.]   From
   this we conclude [that the laws of sacrilege normally cease to apply after
   the blood is actually tossed and the meat is ready] to be eaten.

J. No! [H is talking about the status of the offering if it became disqualified
   before the blood was ready] to be tossed. [The point is that had the animal
   become disqualified after the blood was ready to be tossed, it would already
   have been exempted from the laws of sacrilege. The crucial time is when the
   blood is ready to be tossed.]

K. For what would be the case if [the blood had been ready] to be tossed [when
    the animal was rendered disqualified? Since we consider blood ready to be
    tossed as if it were tossed], the offering would thereby have been exempted
    from the laws of sacrilege. [It follows that the laws of sacrilege cease to
    apply as soon as the blood is ready to be tossed.]

L. If this is so [i.e. that these rulings are meant to teach us about the efect
    of tossing the blood], why does Mishnah go on to teach, "[Disqualified]
    Lesser Holy Things are not subject to the laws of sacrilege"? [Rather than
    make a distinction between Most Holy Things and Lesser Holy Things,] Mishnah
    should distinguish between the case before [the blood is] tossed and the case
    after [the blood is] tossed. [Since this distnction is not made, we must
    conclude that Mishnah here is not concerned with teaching us about the
    disposition of the blood.]

M. [We can respond as follows: This distinction between Most Holy Things and
    Lesser Holy Things] comes to show us that as regards everything that can be
    made subject to the laws of sacrilege [by becoming the priest's property,
    i.e., Lesser Holy Things]--tossing [the blood] properly makes it subject to
    the laws of sacrilege; and as regards everything that is exempted from
    sacrilege [by being made fit for the altar, i.e., Most Holy Things]--tossing
    [the blood] even improperly exempts it from the laws of sacrilege. [The
    point is that what counts is the actual tossing of the blood, not merely the
    blood's readiness to be tossed.]

Under discussion is the effect improperly slaughtering an offering has on
that animal's liability to the laws of sacrilege. Usually, an animal dsignated
as a Most Holy Thing remains subject to the laws of sacrilege until it is either
properly given to the altar or until it is rendered unfit. Mishnah now informs
us that in those cases in which the offering is slaughtered improperly, its meat
remains subject to the laws of sacrilege forever. Thus if I have a ram that I
designated for use use as a whole-offering, that ram becomes subject to the laws
of sacrilege. It would remain so until I slaughtered it and tossed the blood on
the altar, thus rendering it fit for the priests. If I slaughter the animal

improperly, however, I render all further acts inefficacious. Tossing the blood
no longer has the power to render the animal fit for the priest and so exempt
from sacrilege. The authors of the Gemara systematically investigate the
character of such acts of improper slaughtering: Units I-II commenting on M.
1:1A-F, and Unit III taking up M. 1:1G. Unit IV, with its appendix at V, pauses
to resolve a tension discovered between units I-II and III. The tension arises
from the fact that while I-II acknowledge that such improper acts acts of
slaughtering do yield meat that is still subject to the laws of sacrilege, III
argues that such meat is not deemed to be holy at all. It should follow that
such meat is not subject to sacrilege. IV-V resolve the tension by asserting
that the meat is subject to sacrilege only on the basis of a rabbinic decree, not
on the basis of written Scripture. Units VI-VIII turn to a related question,
namely, if any further ritual performed on the disqualified meat can render it
exempt from the laws of sacrilege. This discussion leads us to the theme of M.
1:1/I-O, which is then taken up in unit IX. X-XI goes over the ground of IX,
linking it to the teaching introduced in VI-VIII. So all together we have a
systematic and tightly constructed exploration of Mishnah.

1:2-3

A. [6B] The meat of Most Holy Things which went forth [beyond the veils] before
    the tossing of the blood.

B. R. Eliezer says, "The laws of sacrilege apply to it. And they are not liable
    on its account because of a violation of the laws of refuse, remnant, and
    uncleanness."

C. R. Aqiba says, "The laws of sacrilege do not apply to it. Truly they are
    liable on its account because of violation of the laws of refuse, remnant,
    and uncleanness."

D. Said R. Aqiba, "Now, lo, he who separates a sin-offering which is then lost,
    and separated another in its stead, and afterwards the first turns up, and
    lo, both of them are available--

E. "Is it not so that just as its blood exempts its flesh [from the laws of
    sacrilege], so it exempts the flesh of its fellow?

F. "Now if [the proper tossing of] its blood has exempted the flesh of its
fellow from being subject to the laws of sacrilege, is it not logical that it
would exempt its own flesh?"

M. 1:2

A. The sacrificial parts of Lesser Holy Things which went forth [beyond the
veils] before the tossing of the blood--

B. R. Eliezer says, "The laws of sacrilege do not apply to them. And they are
not liable on their account because of violation of the laws of refuse,
remnant, and uncleanness."

C. R. Aqiba says, "The laws of sacrilege do apply to them. And they are liable
on their account because of violation of laws of refuse, remnant, and
uncleanness."

M. 1:3

I.

A. Why [does Mishnah give rulings] for both [cases separately, i.e., Most Holy
Things in 1:2 and Lesser Holy Things in 1:3]?

B. Both are necessary.

C. For if only the ruling as regards Most Holy Things were stated, I might
[wrongly] conclude that R. Eliezer ruled that the laws of sacrilege apply [to
Most Holy Things because] these become exempt from the laws of sacrilege only
with the proper tossing of the blood, and if the blood is not properly tossed
[as in the case before us, they] do not become exempt.

D. But as regards causing [Lesser Holy Things] to become subject to the laws of
sacrilege, he agrees with R. Aqiba that even improperly tossing the blood
causes them to become subject to the laws of sacrilege.

E. And if only the ruling as regards Lesser Holy Things were stated, I might
[wrongly] conclude that R. Aqiba rules only as regards Lesser Holy Things,
that they become subject to the laws of sacrilege, because these become
subject to the laws of sacrilege even if the blood is improperly tossed.

F. But as regards Most Holy Things [he agrees with Eliezer] that they are not
exempt because improper tossing of the blood does not render them exempt from
the laws of sacrilege.

G. Accordingly [Mishnah provides both cases] to teach us [that in fact, Eliezer and Aqiba disagree on all counts].

II.

A. Said R. Yohanan, "When R. Aqiba ruled that tossing [the blood] has effect [even after] the animal went forth [beyond the veil, M. 1:2C,] he meant only in the case that part of it went forth [beyond the veil]. But [as regards a case in which] all of the animal went forth [beyond the veil], R. Aqiba did not say."

B. R. Assi said to R. Yohanan, "My colleages in Babylonia already taught me [as follows: [7A] 'If one has an improper] thought as regards [an offering that] was lost or burnt up, [that thought disqualifies the whole offering].'

C. "Now this lost or burnt [part] is not present, and yet we learn that intentions [concerning it effect the status of the whole. It follows that if the whole offering, which is present, goes forth beyond the veil, then intentions concerning it can certainly have effect]."

D. Did R. Assi really rule thus [i.e.C]?

E. [No!] [Rather this was what] R. Assi asked R. Yohanan, "What happens if one considers pouring out [the life-blood of an offering] on the following day [rather than on the same day as the slaughtering, as is required]?" [This blood is like the burnt or lost portion of the sacrifice in B insofar as the priest intends to throw it out. Do intentions concerning that blood have any effect on the status of the offering as a whole?]"

F. R. Zera answered, "Did you yourself not teach us [the operative principle when we discussed] alal [unwanted meat trimmings]? Alal, since it has no real value, cannot become unclean, [that is, acts regarding it are entirely irrelevant]. The same should apply to the [life-blood], namely, since it will be poured out as waste, [improper intentions concerning it are irrelevant and so] have no effect."

G. This rule [F], however, stands in apparent contradiction to what is taught regarding [improper intention concerning part of an offering that] is lost or burnt up [B. According to this later rule, improper intentions concerning part of an offering do effect the status of the whole.]

H.   Said Raba, "[There is no contradiction. The rule in B does not refer to a
     part that was actually lost or burnt up, but to a part that] was about to be
     lost or about to be burnt up." [Since that part is still available and is
     integral to the offering, any intention concerning it does have effect. This
     does not contradict E, which concerns the alal, which is actually useless.]

I.   [Reverting to Aqiba's rule in M. 1:2C:] Said R. Papa, "R. Aqiba ruled that
     tossing [the blood] has effect [even after part of the animal] went forth
     [beyond the veil] only if it was the meat that went forth, but if [it was
     part of] the blood that went forth, then tossing [the remainder of the blood]
     has no effect."

J.   It is further taught [as regards the blood]: "If one slaughtered any offering
     with right intention and then [part of] the blood went forth [beyond the
     veil], even if he brings it back inside before tossing it, it is of no avail
     [i.e., once some of the blood has gone forth beyond the veil, subsequent
     tossing of the blood has no effect]. Most Holy Things will still be subject
     to the laws of sacrilege and Lesser Holy Things will still be exempt from the
     laws of sacrilege."

III.

A.   [Turning to M. 1:2D:]   Said R. Aqiba, [He who separates a sin-offering which
     is then lost, and separated another in its stead, and afterwards the first
     turns up and, lo, both of them are available--]:

B.   What does this ruling mean?

C.   Said R. Eliezer, "When R. Aqiba ruled [that tossing of the blood of the
     original animal makes available its meat and the meat of its replacement, he
     meant this only if both were slaughtered] at the same moment. But if one
     was slaughtered after the other, R. Aqiba did not hold [that the meat of the
     second offering is affected by tossing the blood of the first]."

D.   It is taught [on Tannaitic authority]:

E.   Said R. Simeon, "As I was walking to Kfar Pagi [Porusch: Beth Page, near
     Jerusalem], I came across a certain old man who said to me, 'Did R. Aqiba
     used to say that tossing [the blood of a Lesser Holy Thing] has effect [after
     part of the animal] went forth [beyond the veil]?'[T. 1:5]

E.   "I said to him, 'Yes.'

F.   "When I arrived and related these matters to my colleagues in Galilee, they
     said to me, 'But is not [the animal thereby] disqualified? How can the
     sprinkling make [the meat] acceptable [to the priest]?'

G.   "When I left and related these matters to R. Aqiba, he said to me, 'My son.
     Have you not ruled this same way [yourself]?

H.   "'Look, suppose someone designates [an animal] as a sin-offering and it gets
     lost, and he designates a second in its stead and then the first one is found
     so that both stand ready. Both are subject to the laws of sacrilege. If he
     slaughters them and their blood is collected in bowls, both [are still]
     subject to the laws of sacrilege. [7B] If the blood of one of them [is then
     properly] tossed, would you not agree that since the blood exempts the meat
     [of the beast from which it came] from the laws of sacrilege [cf. M.1:2F],
     it should also exempt the flesh of its fellow from the laws of sacrilege?
     And if it can save its fellow from the laws of sacrilege, even though that
     beast is disqualified, does it not follow logically that it should save,
     [that is, exempt from the laws of sacrifice, the meat] of its own animal.'"

I.   Said Resh Laqish in the name of R. Oshaiah, "R. Aqiba gave an elusive answer
     to the student. [According to C, he rules that tossing the blood of one
     beast exempts from the laws of sacrilege both its own meat and the meat of
     its substitute,] if both are slaughtered at the same moment, but not [if they
     were slaughtered] one after the other. [In D-H], however, since [the meat
     went forth beyond the veil and] became disqualified, what difference would it
     make if [the animal and its substitute were slaughtered] at the same moment
     or one after the other?" [In all events, tossing the blood would have no
     effect.]

J.   Said R. Yohanan to Resh Laqish, "[It makes a difference because if they are
     slaughtered separately, they are regarded separately, such that if part of
     one went forth it does not effect the status of the other.]

K.   "And you yourself hold this same view: if one separated two guilt-offerings,
     one as a guarantee for the other, and then slaughtered both and [tossed the
     blood of one] and then brought the meat of the other up to the altar before
     tossing [its blood] -- would you not agree that the meat that went up [to the
     altar] must come down [until its blood is tossed]?

L.   "Now if you regard the meat of both offerings as belonging to one body--why
     should the meat that went up come down? For did not Ulla say, 'Meat of
     Lesser Holy Things which comes up to the altar before the blood is tossed,
     does not come down because it becomes the property of the altar [as soon as
     the blood is tossed'? Since you rule that the meat comes down, you clearly
     hold that each animal is treated separately--just as Aqiba does]."

M.   [Resh Laqish could not respond to this and so] kept silent.

N.   Said R. Yohanan, "I have pulled out the rug from under the feet of that
     youngster [i.e., Resh Laqish]."

Unit I asks about the general formulation of Mishnah's ruling, wondering in
particular why Most Holy Things and Lesser Holy Things are treated separately.
The reason, we are told, is to highlight the systematic difference between
Eliezer's view and Aqiba's view. Having said this, the Gemara turns, in units II
and III, to an investigation of Aqiba's rulings. Unit II looks briefly at M. 1:3
while unit III develops a complicated critique of M. 1:2. The Gemara thus
proceeds from a direct comment on Mishnah's language to a more abstract
reflection on the meaning of the ruling.

1:4

A.   A deed having to do with the blood in the case of Most Holy Things produces a
     ruling which is lenient and one which is stringent.

B.   But in the case of Lesser Holy Things, the whole [tendency] is to impose a
     stringent ruling.

C.   How so?

D.   Most Holy Things before the tossing of the blood--

E.   The laws of sacrilege apply [both] to the sacrificial parts and to the meat
     [which is for the priests. This is the stringency].

F.   After the tossing of the blood, the laws of sacrilege apply [only] to the
     sacrificial parts, but they do not apply to the meat. [This is the
     leniency.]

G. On account of this and on account of that are they liable because of
   violation of the laws of refuse, remnant, and uncleanness.

H. [B. adds:] It turns out that a deed having to do with the blood in the case
   of Most Holy Things produces a ruling which is lenient and one which is
   stringent.

I. But in the case of Lesser Holy Things, the whole [tendency] is to impose a
   stringent ruling.

J. How so?

K. Lesser Holy Things before the tossing of the blood--

L. The laws of sacrilege do not apply either to the sacrificial parts or to the
   meat. [The stringency lies in the fact that the laws of sacrilege apply to
   nothing at all until the blood is tossed.]

M. After the tossing of the blood, the laws of sacrilege apply to the
   sacrificial parts, but they do not apply to the meat. [The stringency here is
   that an item that was once exempt from the laws of sacrilege is now rendered
   liable to them.]

N. On account of this and on account of that they are liable because of
   violation of the laws of refuse, remnant and uncleanness.

O. It turns out that a deed having to do with the blood in the case of Most Holy
   Things produces a ruling which is lenient and one which is stringent, but in
   the case of Lesser Holy Things, the whole [tendency] is to impose a stringent
   ruling.

I.

A. [The Mishnah-passage] teaches: [After the tossing of the blood,] the laws
   of sacrilege apply to the sacrificial parts, but they do not apply to the
   meat [M. 1:4F]:

B. [Since this states only that the laws of sacrilege do not apply, I should
   conclude that while] the laws of sacrilege do not apply, [the meat
   nonetheless remains] prohibited [to the priests].

C. [This conclusion does not follow.] Why [should the meat be prohibited
   since], lo, it is the property of the priest?

D. [Actually this wording should create] no such problem. [Rather] since the
   author said in the first clause [= M. 1:4E], "The laws of sacrilege apply,"
   he used [a parallel phrase] for the later clause, namely, "The laws of
   sacrilege do not apply." [The wording bears no other implication.]

E. I respond by citing the second half [of this teaching, which is not worded so
   as to preserve a literary parallelism]: But in the case of Lesser Holy
   Things, the whole [tendency] is to impose a stringent ruling--how so? The
   meat of Lesser Holy Things before the tossing of the blood--the laws of
   sacrilege do not apply either to it or to the sacrificial parts, and one is
   not liable on their account because of violation of the laws of refuse,
   remnant and uncleanness. But after the blood is tossed, the laws of
   sacrilege apply to the sacrificial parts, but not to the meat [cf. M. 1:4H-
   M]. [Thus D's claim that the framers of Mishnah are committed to preserving
   literary parallelisms is shown to be false.]

F. [And, in fact, this Mishnah-passage clearly implies that] while the laws of
   sacrilege do not apply to the offering, the meat is nonetheless prohibited
   [to the priest, just as B has said].

G. But why [should the meat be prohibited since], lo, it is the property of the
   donor?

H. [R. Hanina reconciles these two positions.] Said R. Hanina, "[The
   prohibition applies, but only to meat] that had gone forth [beyond the
   sanctuary and was then brought back in]. [This meat is prohibited to the
   priests, in line with B and E-F. In all other cases, the meat is avaiable to
   the priests, in line with C-D and G.]"

I. [This ruling has support, for it is also] the view of R. Aqiba, for R. Aqiba
   said, "Tossing the blood of [Lesser Holy Things] that went forth [beyond the
   veil] qualifies the meat [as a valid offering] for burning, [8A] but it does
   not render the meat fit to be eaten. [That is, such meat is prohibited to
   the priests, cf. M. 1:3.]

The Gemara searches for the implication behind Mishnah's formulation of its
rulings. B reads Mishnah's language in its most narrow sense: once the blood of

Most Holy Things is tossed, the laws of sacrilege cease to apply but nothing else changes. This means, for exammple, that the meat still may not be eaten by the priests. C-D rightly challenge this as impossible. After all, the whole point is for the priests to consume the sacred meat. E-F then reiterate B's point, citing the second half of Mishnah's passage. This is in turn subject to the same challenge, now at G. The two possibilities are reconciled by Hanina at H-I.

2:1

A. The sin-offering of fowl--

B. The laws of sacrilege apply to it once it [the bird] has been sanctified
    [designated as a sin-offering].

C. [When] its head has been severed, it is rendered fit to be made invalid by a
    Tebul Yom and by one whose rites of atonement have not yet been completed and
    by being left overnight.

D. [When] its blood has been tossed, they are liable on its account because of a
    violation of the laws of refuse, remnant and uncleanness.

E. And the laws of sacrilege do not apply to it [any longer].

I.

A. [This Mishnah-passage] teaches: [When its head has been severed,] it is
    rendered fit to be made invalid by a Tebul Yom and by one whose rites of
    atonement have not yet been completed and by being left overnight [M. 2:1C].

B. [This means that the sin-offering] is itself rendered disqualified, but is
    not rendered able to pass on uncleanness [to other things].

C. With [whose view of matters] does our Mishnah-passage agree?

D. [It agrees] with [the view of] sages, for this is what is taught:

E. Abba Saul says, "A Tebul Yom [8B] is unclean in the first degree as regards
    Holy Things [rendering them unclean in the second degree and capable of
    conveying uncleanness in the third degree] [T. Toh. 1:4A]."

F. And R. Meir says, "[A Tebul Yom] renders Holy Things unclean [in the third
    degree and capable of conveying uncleanness in the fourth degree] and renders
    heave-offering invalid [that is, unclean but unable to pass uncleanness on to
    other things]." [In contrast to both of these, our Mishnah-passage claims
    that Holy Things are not able to convey uncleaness.]

G. But sages say, "Just as [the Tebul Yom] renders invalid drink [in the status
   of] heave-offering and food [in the status of] heave-offering [such that
   these are unclean but unable to convey uncleanness to other things], so too
   does he render invalid consecrated food and consecrated drink."

H. Said Raba, "[The sages view combines the other two. They] agree with Abba
   Saul that [the Tebul Yom renders] consecrated foods [unclean], and as such
   they treat the Tebul Yom as though he suffers first-degree uncleanness.

I. "[And they agree] with R. Meir [that the Tebul Yom bears the level of
   uncleanness of food] unclean in the second degree [and as such they deem that
   which he touches as not capable of conveying uncleanness to other foods].

J. "For our sages hold that since [the Tebul Yom] immersed, his uncleanness is
   diluted and [what he touches] is like something rendered invalid [i.e., which
   cannot pass on uncleanness] and is not like something rendered unclean [which
   does pass on uncleanness]."

II.

A. When its blood has been tossed, they are liable on its account [because of a
   violation of the laws of refuse, remnant or uncleanness] and the laws of
   sacrilege do not apply to it [any longer]. [M. 2:1D-E]

B. [The reason that the laws of sacrilege are specifically mentioned is to tell
   us that] although the laws of sacrilege no longer apply, there is still a
   prohibition [against the priest eating the meat].

C. [We again challenge this assertion (see I.B. to M. 1:4).] Why should this
   be? Is it not the case that [the meat] becomes the property of the priest
   [once the blood is tossed]?

D. Said R. Hanina, "[The rule at B refers only to meat that had] gone forth
   [beyond the veil. That meat is no longer subject to sacrilege, but may not be
   eaten by the priests.]"

E. But was it not R. Aqiba who said, "The tossing [of blood] has effect [even on
   meat] that has gone forth [beyond the veil, implying that such meat does
   indeed become available to the priests]"?

F. [In fact, the ruling of B does not contradict Aqiba. Tossing the blood does have effect, in that it renders the meat exempt from the laws of sacrilege, but this meat] nonetheless may not be eaten.

III.

A. Said R. Huna in the name of Rab, "Improperly squeezing out [the blood] of a bird brought as a sin-offering does not prevent [the rest of the ritual from being properly carried out];

B. "for Rab taught, '[M. 2:1D says only,] <u>When its blood has been tossed,</u> [not when the blood has been <u>squeezed out</u>].'"

C. R. Adda bar Ahava said [in the name of] Rab, "[Improperly] squeezing [the blood] from a bird brought as a sin-offering does prevent [the rest of the ritual from being properly carried out];

D. "for Rab taught, '[M. 2:2 says,] <u>When its blood has been squeezed out. . .</u>, [thus explicitly requiring that the blood be properly squeezed out].'"

E. Come and hear: [Leviticus 5:9b states,] "The rest of the blood [in the carcass] is to be squeezed out at the base of the altar. [It is a sin-offering.]"

F. This is in perfect accord with the view of Adda bar Ahava [who says that the blood must be squeezed out] for, lo, Scripture [itself says,] "The rest of the blood [in the carcass] is to be squeezed out at the base of the altar; it is [then a valid] sin-offering."

G. How does R. Huna [interpret this verse]?

H. [He interprets the words] "The rest" as does the school of R. Ishmael [namely,] if there is blood remaining [that blood <u>should</u> be squeezed out, but does not <u>have</u> to be].

I. [And] how [does R. Huna interpret the phrase] "It is [then a valid] sin-offering"?

J. [He reads this phrase] in light of the first [clause, namely, Lev. 5:9a, which reads, "He shall toss some of the blood of the sin-offering on the side of the altar." That is, properly tossing some of the blood renders the offering a valid sin-offering. What happens to the rest is irrelevant.]

K. Said R. Aha the son of Raba to R. Ashi, "[R. Huna is wrong when he says that
    we do not need to squeeze out all of the blood remaining in the carcass. We
    must] rather [interpret Mishnah in light of what we find in Lev. 2:2-3]:
    'What is left [of the meal-offering belongs to Aaron. . .' This passage
    shows that what happens to the left over meal is significant.] Likewise
    here, blood that is left over [in the carcass is significant. It must be
    properly squeezed out as Adda bar Ahava has said.]

L. "And if you should argue [the reverse, namely: just as the remaining blood
    is of no consequence] so too is [the left over meal of no consequence, I can
    prove you wrong].

M. [9A] "For is it not taught [in Lev. 2:2, 'He shall take a handful] of its
    fine flour and its oil and all of its frankincense'? [This means that] there
    should be lacking none of its flour or its oil or its frankincense. [That
    is, all of these ingredients are significant and must be disposed of
    properly.]"

N. They say [in reply], "It is written subsequently [in Lev. 2:10], 'The rest
    [of the meal-offering].' This seemingly extra use [of the word 'rest'
    indicating that only left over meal is of consequence, not left over blood.
    Huna's view that the leftover blood is of no consequence still stands.]"

O. Samuel's father and R. Abin responded to R. Huna['s view that the left over
    blood is of no consequence]. "A bird brought for a sin-offering and a bird
    brought for a burnt-offering are alike in that [if they are properly killed
    by] having their heads pinched off and their blood is [properly] squeezed
    out while [the priest forms the intention of eating the meat] outside its
    [proper] place, they are disqualified as pasul and [the one who misuses them]
    is not subject to extirpation.

P. "[They are also alike in that if they are properly slaughtered and their
    blood is properly squeezed out while the priest forms the intention of eating
    the meat] outside its [proper] time, they are unfit as piggul and [the one
    who misuses them] is subject to extirpation.

Q. "Now in all these cases, [properly] squeezing out the blood is required."
    [From this we conclude that the proper disposition of the blood is
    important.]

R. Having raised [this objection], he then explained it away. [The law is in
fact different] in each case. [While for both cases the bird's neck must be
pinched, it is only the blood of the sin-offering that must be totally
squeezed out, not the blood of the burnt-offering.]

IV.

A. [Reverting to the] body of [the discussion]: the school of R. Ishmael
taught, "If any blood remains," [implying that the offering is acceptable
even if blood remains in the carcass].

B. But did not the school of R. Ishmael teach elsewhere that the remaining blood
[must properly be squeezed out or the offering is] rendered disqualified
[Cf. Zeb. 42a]?

C. Said R. Papa, "[The disagreement] between these two views concerns [only] a
fowl brought as a sin-offering, [and] this disagreement goes back to a
dispute between Tannaitic authorities as to what R. Ishmael had said." [cf.
IIIH]

This commentary consists of three parts, each with a distinct interest. Unit
I is concerned with identifying the authority who stands behind the rule of M.
2:1A-C. Unit II focusses attention on M.2:1D-E, bringing to it the same question
that was debated in conjunction with Mishnah 1:4, namely, whether or not tossing
the blood renders the meat available to the priests. Units III-IV, finally,
introduce a complicated problem associated with the disposition of any blood
remaining in the bird after its blood has been properly tossed. According to
Huna, the disposition of this blood is of no consequence since the rite has
already been properly carried out. Rab, on the other hand, holds that all the
blood in the animal is significant and so holds that all of its must be disposed
of in the correct manner. IV concludes this discussion by showing that the issue
was already debated by the Tanaitic authorities.

2:2-8

A.   The burnt-offering of fowl--

B.   The laws of sacrilege apply to it once it has been sanctified.

C.   [When] its head has been severed, it is rendered fit to be made invalid by a
     Tebul Yom and by one whose rites of atonement have not yet been completed and
     by being left overnight.

D.   [When] its blood has been squeezed out, they are liable on its account
     because of violation of the laws of refuse, remnant, and uncleanness.

E.   And the laws of sacrilege apply to it until it is taken out to the ash-heap.

M. 2:2

A.   Cows which are to be burned and goats which are to be burned--

B.   the laws of sacrilege apply to them once they have been sanctified.

C.   [When] they have been slaughtered, they are rendered fit to be made invalid
     by a Tebul Yom and by one whose rites of atonement have not yet been
     completed and by being left overnight.

D.   [When] their blood has been tossed, they are liable on their account because
     of violation of the laws of refuse, remnant, and uncleanness.

E.   And the laws of sacrilege apply to them in the ash-heap until the meat is
     reduced to cinders.

M. 2:3

A.   The burnt-offering--

B.   the laws of sacrilege apply to it once it has been sanctified.

C.   [When] it has been slaughtered, it is rendered fit to be made invalid by a
     Tebul Yom and by one whose rites of atonement have not yet been completed and
     by being left overnight.

D.   [When] its blood has been tossed, they are liable on its account because of
     violation of the laws of refuse, remnant, and uncleanness.

E.   And the laws of sacrilege do not apply to its hide.

F.   But the laws of sacrilege do apply to the meat until it is taken out to the
     ash-heap.

M. 2:4

A. A sin-offering, and a guilt-offering, and communal sacrifices of peace-
   offerings--

B. the laws of sacrilege apply to them once they have been sanctified.

C. [When] they have been slaughtered, they are rendered fit to be made invalid
   by a Tebul Yom and by one whose rites of atonement have not yet been
   completed and by being left overnight.

D. [When] their blood has been tossed, they are liable on their account because
   of violation of the laws of refuse, remnant, and uncleanness.

E. The laws of sacrilege do not apply to the meat.

F. But the laws of sacrilege apply to the sacrificial parts until they are taken
   out to the ash-heap.

M. 2:5

A. The two loaves--

B. the laws of sacrilege apply to them once they have been sanctified.

C. [When] they have formed a crust in the oven, they have been rendered fit to
   be made invalid by a Tebul Yom and by one whose rites of atonement have not
   yet been completed and to have slaughtered the animal-sacrifice [which
   pertains to them (Lev. 23:18)] on their account.

D. [When] the blood of the lambs has been tossed, they are liable on their
   account because of violation of the laws of refuse, remnant, and
   uncleanness.

E. But sacrilege does not apply to them.

M. 2:6

A. The show bread--

B. the laws of sacrilege apply to it once it has been sanctified.

C. [When] it has formed a crust in the oven, it has been rendered fit to be made
   invalid by a Tebul Yom and by one whose rites of atonement has not yet been
   completed and to be laid out on the table.

D. [When] the dishes of incense have been offered, they are liable on its

account because of violation of the laws of refuse, remnant, and
uncleanness.

E.   And sacrilege does not pertain to it [any longer].

                            M. 2:7

A.   Meal-offerings--

B.   the laws of sacrilege apply to them once they have been sanctified.

C.   [When] they have been sanctified in a utensil, they are rendered fit to be
     made invalid by a Tebul Yom and by one whose rites of atonement have not yet
     been completed and by being left overnight.

D.   [When] the handful [of the meal-offering] has been offered, they are liable
     on their account because of violation of the laws of refuse, remnant, and
     uncleanness.

E.   And the laws of sacrilege do not apply to the residue. But the laws of
     sacrilege apply to the handful [of the meal-offering itself] until it is
     taken out to the ash-heap.

                            M. 2:8

I.

A.   It has been stated [on Amoraic authority], "As regards one who derives
     benefit from the ashes piled on the altar, Rab said, 'The laws of sacrilege
     do not apply [i.e., the ashes are not holy]';
     but R. Yohanan said, 'The laws of sacrilege do apply.' [i.e. that the ashes
     are holy]."

B.   Now everyone agree that the laws of sacrilege apply [to the ashes] before
     they are collected [from the altar, since the collection and removal of the
     ashes is required by (Lev. 6:3)].

C.   About what do they disagree? About [the status of the ashes] after their
     collection and removal. Rab said, "The laws of sacrilege do not apply
     because, lo, all requirements [connected with them] have been done."

D.   And R. Yohanan says, "The laws of sacrilege continue to apply because
     Scripture states [that after the ashes are collected and removed] 'the priest
     is to don his linen garment...(Lev. 6:3).' Since [the priest] must [wear]

his sacramental clothes [when handling the ash], they must still be in their state of holiness."

E. Now we have learned [in M. 2:2E]: the laws of sacrilege apply to it until [its ashes] are taken out to the ash-heap. This seems [to pose] a difficulty for Rab [who rules that the law of sacrilege ceases to apply as soon as the ash is gathered together on the altar].

F. Rab could reply [that Mishnah does not mean until the ash is actually taken to the ash-heap, but only] when it is ready to go to the ash-heap [i.e., when it is gathered together].

G. [9B] They raised [the following] objection [to Rab]: "We have learned [in M. Zeb. 9:6]: And any of them [i.e., the invalid offerings enumerated in M. Zeb. 9:5] which burst from off the altar, one should not put them back. And so [is the rule for] a coal which burst from off the altar, one should not put it back!

H. "[This seems to say that if the coal burst off the fire, but] stayed on the altar, they do return it [to the fire]. This appears to be fine from R. Yohanan's [point of view since he holds that the ashes gathered from the fire continue to be holy]. But it is a difficulty for Rab [who holds that ash removed from the fire is no longer holy]."

I. Let Rab reply to you [as follows: You cannot draw an analogy between the coal mentioned in M. Zeb. and the ashes to which my rule applies]. The coal [of M. Zeb.] is different in that it still has substance [and so can carry a status of holiness. The ash, I have in mind, however, has no substance and so is of no consequence.]

J. There are those who state the whole matter in this way: The reason [for returning the coal] is that it has substance [and so carries a holy status. It follows] that ash, which has no substance [and thus can carry no holy status, is of no consequence] even if it is on the altar. [Therefore] the laws of sacrilege do not apply to it.

K. Now [J] appears to be fine from Rab's [point of view since he holds that ashes removed from the fire are of no consequence]. But it is a difficulty for R. Yohanan [who holds that such ashes are still in a holy status].

L.   Then let R. Yohanan reply to you [as follows]: The rule [that we return to
     the fire items that have burst out of the fire and onto the altar] applies
     even to ashes. The reason that coals are specifically mentioned is to teach
     us that even coals, which have substance need not be returned [to the fire]
     if they burst off the altar [entirely. But if either coal or ash remain on
     the altar, they must be pushed back into the fire.]

II.

A.   It has been stated [in the name of Amoraic masters]:

B.   "As for one who derives benefit from the meat of Most Holy Things before the
     blood is tossed or from the sacrificial parts of Lesser Holy Things after the
     blood is tossed—Rab said, '[The value of] what he took for [personal]
     benefit is to be repaid [to the Temple] as a voluntary contribution.' But
     Levi said, 'He should bring a [new] item that [will go] entirely to the
     altar.'"

C.   [The following] was taught in accord with Levi's view: "In the case of a
     sacrilege [of this sort], to whom [does the penalty-payment] go? Those who
     argue before the sages say, '[We should use the penalty-payment] to bring
     something that [will go] entirely to the altar.'

D.   "What would such a thing be? Incense, [for example]."

E.   [The following] was taught in accord with Rab's [view]: "[As regards] one who
     derives [personal] benefit from money [set aside to buy] a sin-offering or a
     guilt-offering—[if he makes repayment] before he offered his sin-offering,
     he should add [a fifth to the original value and spend the whole on] a sin-
     offering; if before he has offered his guilt-offering, he should add [a fifth
     to the original value and spend the whole on] a guilt-offering. [If, on the
     other hand, he makes repayment] after he offered his sin-offering [so that
     the repaid money can not be used to towards a sin-offering], he should take
     [the repayment money and toss it into] the Dead Sea [so that it will never be
     used for secular purposes; if] after he had offered a guilt-offering, the
     [money] is to be given to the Temple as a voluntary contribution.

F. "As for one who derives benefit from Most Holy Things before the blood is
    tossed or from the sacrificial portions of Lesser Holy Things after the blood
    is tossed—[the value of] what he took for [personal] benefit is to be repaid
    [to the Temple] as a voluntary contribution [according to the following
    schedule]:

G. "[repayment for the misuse of] an offering [designated] for the altar is
    [used to buy items] for the altar;

H. "[repayment for the misuse of] an offering [designated] for the Temple upkeep
    is [used for] Temple upkeep;

I. "[repayment for the misuse of an] offering [designated for] public [worship
    is used to buy offerings for] public freewill offerings."

J. [An objection is raised. The rule in G seems to] contradict [the rule in
    E],

K. [for E states, "if he makes repayment] before he offered his sin-offering, he
    should add [a fifth to the original value and use the whole amount] to bring
    a sin-offering. . . ; if after he offered his sin-offering, he should take
    [the money and toss it] into the Dead Sea." [That is, E makes a distinction
    between repayment made before the sin-offering is completed, and after the
    sin-offering is completed.]

L. [G, however,] teaches, "[Repayment for] an offering [designated] for the
    altar, [such as a sin-offering] is [used to buy other items] for the altar,"
    — [apparently] irrespective of whether or not the donor has already
    completed his atonement [by offering a sin-offering]."

M. [We can reconcile E and G by ascribing them to different authorities.] The
    first rule [E] is that of R. Simeon, who said, "[In the case of] all sin-
    offerings [which comes to hand] after their donor has already atoned [by
    offering another animal]—this first animal is left to die, [this being the
    equivalent of tossing consecrated money into the Dead Sea]."

M. [10A] The last rule [G] is that of the rabbis.

N. [The following tradition supports this explanation:] Said R. Gebiha of Be
    Ketil to R. Ashi, "Thus did Abayye say: 'The first rule [E] is that of R.
    Simeon, and the last rule [G] is that of our rabbis.'"

III.

A. Said Raba, "All agree that if one takes for one's personal use the meat of
    Most Holy Things which had been rendered unclean before the tossing of the
    blood, or the sacrificial portions of Lesser Holy Things [which had been
    rendered unclean] after they have been placed on the altar, this one is
    exempt [from having to repay the value of what he took]."

B. But this is obvious! What loss [has the altar suffered? Unclean Most Holy
    Things can not be placed on the altar at all and Lesser Holy Things once
    placed on the altar have satisfied the altar's demand. Since in either case
    the altar is not deprived of anything it would otherwise have, there is
    nothing to repay.]

C. [It is necessary to state the rule in B for the following reason:] Otherwise
    you might wrongly conclude that the priest is [still] obligated to burn the
    meat of Most Holy Things which had been rendered unclean; or is [still]
    obligated to turn over [on the altar fire] the sacrificial parts of Lesser
    Holy Things [which had become unclean]. Accordingly [this ruling is stated]
    to tell us that no [further obligation regarding this unclean meat exists].

D. Said Raba [to Rab], "Concerning what you said [in II. E], namely, '[As
    regards one who derives personal benefit from money set aside to buy a sin-
    offering . . . , if he makes repayment] after he offered his sin-offering],
    he should throw [the repayment money into the Dead Sea]' -- this applies only
    if he realized before he offered the other sin-offering [that he misused the
    original money]. But if he realized [his mistake] only after he offered the
    other sin-offering, [then the repayment] becomes a freewill offering. [That
    is, Raba is saying that if one realized that he had misused the consecrated
    money only after he offered the sin-offering, then the repayment money should
    not be tossed into the Dead Sea, as Rab said, but should go toward a freewill
    offering.]

E. "What is the reason? One ought not set aside consecrated items that to begin
    with must be destroyed."

M. 2:2-8 review the various kinds of offerings brought to the altar, defining
the point in the sacrificial process of each when a shift in status occurs. For

purposes of our Gemara, the important shift occurs when the animal or meal becomes exempt from the laws of sacrilege. For birds and animals, this occurs when the animal is completely reduced to ash which is then removed from the altar. At issue in unit I is to determine the status of this ash. Is this ash holy until it is taken to the ash-heap, or is it no longer consecrated since the altar fire has completely transformed it? Gemara determines that the ash remains holy until it is fully disposed of. II and III do not comment on our Mishnah-passage directly, but turn to a related issue, namely, how one is to make restitution for having misappropriated a sacrificial item. Unit II takes up a straightforward case. Someone has set aside money for a sin-offering and then inadvertently used that money for a secular purpose. When he realizes his mistake, he must replace the money (plus a penalty of an added fifth) and use it to buy a new sin-offering. If, however, he realized the mistake only after having already offered a sin-offering, then this solution will not do; there is no call for a second sin-offering. The person thus must reimburse the altar in some other way. III takes up the same theme, but with an added complication. Consecrated material is used inadvertently for ordinary purposes after it has been rendered unclean. Consecrated meat that is rendered unclean can, of course, not be placed on the altar. Now the question is since the meat is in any case unfit for the altar, does the person need to reimburse the altar at all.

2:9

A. The handful, the frankincense, the incense, the meal-offerings of priests, and the meal-offering of the anointed priest, and the meal-offering which accompanies drink-offerings [M. Zeb. 4:3]—

B. the laws of sacrilege apply to them once they have been sanctified.

C. [When] they have been sanctified in a utensil, they are rendered fit to be made invalid by a Tebul Yom and by one whose rites of atonement have not yet been completed and by being left overnight.

D. And they are liable on their account because of violation of the laws of remnant and because of violation of the laws of uncleanness.

E. But the prohibition of refuse does not apply to them.

F. This is the general principle: For whatever is subject to that which renders
    the offering permitted are they not liable on account of violation of the
    laws of refuse, remnant, and uncleanness until that which renders the
    offering permitted has been properly offered.

G. And for whatever is not subject to that which renders the offering permitted,
    once it has been sanctified in a utensil are they liable on account of the
    violation of the laws of remnant, and on account of violation of the laws of
    uncleanness.

H. But the law of refuse does not apply to it [at all].

I.

A. [10B] What is the basis for this ruling [i.e., that the laws of uncleanness
    apply to items which do not depend on a prior act to become permitted as soon
    as they are sanctified in a vessel, M. 2:9 G-H]?

B. [This ruling is made for the following reason.] Our rabbis taught:

C. "I might have thought that the laws of uncleanness apply only to items which
    depend on a prior act to be permitted. [This would seem to follow on
    strictly] logical [grounds, through a comparison of the laws of uncleanness,
    which are less strict, with the laws of disqualification, which are more
    strict]. Disqualification occurs through a single act of awareness, and its
    restitution is a fixed amount and [these penalties] are not suspended if the
    whole [community ate the meat]. Nonetheless this status applies only to
    items that depend on a prior act to be permitted. [But as regards the less
    strict laws of] uncleanness, which occur [only] through two [acts of
    awareness—i.e., awareness that one is unclean and awareness that one is
    eating holy food while unclean—] and its restitution is based on a sliding
    scale [depending on the means of the individual] and [these penalties] are
    suspended if the whole [community ate the meat while unclean—such as a
    Passover], it would seem to follow that this status surely would apply only
    to items that depend on a prior act to be permitted. [For this reason,
    Mishnah must specifically state that uncleanness applies even to items that
    do not depend on a prior act.]"

D. [A further reason is that] Scripture says, "Say to them: should anyone of
    your seed throughout your generations approach ('sr yqrb) [while in a state
    of uncleanness any holy thing which the Children of Israel have dedicated to
    the Lord—that soul shall be cut off from before Me. I am the Lord (Lev.
    22:3).]"

E. Here Scripture speaks about every holy things [being subject to the laws of
    uncleanness].

F. I might falsely conclude from this that [people] are liable for rendering
    [Holy Things] unclean as soon as [they touch them].

G. Therefore Scripture says, "approach," [meaning that Holy Things are liable to
    becoming unclean only when they are ready to approach the altar]."

H. [This is explained by R. Eleazar as follows:] R. Eleazar said, "Is it indeed
    true that one who merely touches any Holy Thing deserves [to be cut off?
    Surely not! Then] how [are we to interpret M. 2:9 G–H]?

I. "[We interpret it as follows: As regards] any sacrifice which depends on a
    prior act to be permitted, one is not subject to [being cut off for touching
    it] until that prior act has been done. And [as regards] any sacrifice
    which does not depend on a prior act to be permitted, one is not subject to
    [being cut off for touching it] until it has been sanctified in a vessel [and
    so rendered ready for the altar]."

Mishnah sets forth two criteria for determining when a sacred animal is
subject to the laws of uncleanness. For an animal that requires some prior act
to render the meat permitted for the altar -- sprinkling the blood of a peace-
offering, for example -- that act must first be performed. If no such prior act
is required, the animal is liable as soon as it is sanctified in the proper
vessel.   The Gemara wants to discover the basis for this later rule.   It is able
to find a logical reason (A–C) as well as a Scriptural warrant (D-I).

3:1

A. (1) The offspring of a sin-offering, and (2) the substitute of a sin-offering, and (3) a sin-offering, the owner of which died, are left to die.

B. [The sin-offering] (1) which became superannuated, or (2) which was lost, or (3) which turned out to be blemished,

C. if [this is] after the owner has effected atonement,

D. is left to die, and does not impart the status of substitute [to an animal designated in its stead].

E. And it is not available for enjoyment, but is not subject to the law of sacrilege.

F. [11A] And if [this is] before the owner has effected atonement,

G. it is put out to pasture until it suffers a blemish, then it is sold, and with its proceeds he [the owner] brings another, and it does impart the status of substitute [to an animal designated in its stead].

H. And it is subject to the laws of sacrilege.

I.

A. What is the difference between the first [case, M. 3:1A] in which no distinction is made [as to whether or not the owner has effected atonement] and the second [case, B-H] in which [such] a distinction is made?

B. In the first case the matter is straightforward. [The offspring of a sin-offering, etc. are always deemed holy even though they are not fully in the status of a sin-offering. They thus are always left to die.] But in the second case, the matter is not so straightforward [since if the owner has not yet offered a sin-offering, the listed animals must be replaced].

II.

A. This [same Mishnah-passage is cited] in connection with the law of substitutes [i.e., M. Tem. 4:1. Why is it repeated verbatim here]?

B. It is taught there because [it deals with the topic] of substitution. It is
    taught here because [it deals with the topic] of sacrilege.

Talmud accounts for the wording of Mishnah's law (I) and then for its
inclusion in this tractate(II).

3:2

A. He who sets aside coins for his Nazirite-offering[s] [Num. 6:14: a he-lamb as
    a burnt-offering, a ewe-lamb as a sin-offering, a ram as a peace-offering]--

B. they [the coins] are not available for benefit.

C. But they [the coins] are not subject to the laws of sacrilege, because they
    [the sacrifices] are appropriate to be offered wholly as peace-offerings
    [Lesser Holy Things, not subject to sacrilege before the blood is tossed].

D. [If] he died,

E. [if] they were not designated [for their particular respective purposes],
    they fall [to the Temple-treasury] as a freewill-offering.

F. [If] they were designated [for their particular, respective purposes], the
    money set aside for the sin-offering is to go to the Salt Sea.

G. They are not available for benefit, but they are not subject to the laws of
    sacrilege.

H. [With] the money set aside for the burnt-offering they are to bring a burnt-
    offering.

I. And [with] the money set aside for peace-offerings, they are to bring peace-
    offerings.

J. And they are eaten for one day [M. Zeb. 5:6] and do not require bread [Num.
    6:19].

I.

A. To this Resh Laqish objected: [If Mishnah 3:2 A-C rules thus,] it should
    also rule: "one who sets aside coins for bird-offerings--they [the coins] are
    not available for benefit, but they are not subject to the laws of sacrilege,
    because they may be used to buy [offerings that are not subject to the laws
    of sacrilege such as] turtledoves which are not old enough or doves which
    are too old."

B. Raba said, "[This does not follow]. Torah does rule that one may bring a
    peace-offering with the undesignated money, [hence the ruling of M. 3:2 A-C,
    that the coins are not subject to the laws of sacrilege]. Does Torah rule,
    however, that one may bring turtledoves that are too young [or doves that are
    too old] and so are unsuitable for the altar? [Of course not! The point is
    that any money designated to buy a bird-offering must be used to buy one that
    is valid, and thus subject to the laws of sacrilege.]"

Resh Laqish believes he has found an implication in Mishnah that leads to his
conclusion in A. B rejects his argument.

3:3

A. R. Simeon says, "Blood is subject to a lenient law at the outset and to a
    strict law at the end, [and] the drink-offerings are subject to a strict rule
    at the outset and to a lenient rule at the end.

B. "The blood at the outset: the laws of sacrilege do not apply to it. [This is
    the leniency.]

C. "[When] it has gone forth to the Qidron Brook, the laws of sacrilege apply to
    it. [This is the stringency.]

D. Drink offerings at the outset: the laws of sacrilege apply to them. [This is
    a stringency.]

E. "[When] they have gone forth to the pits, the laws of sacrilege do not apply
    to them." [Thus the law becomes more lenient.]

I.

A. Our rabbis taught [on Tannaitic authority]:

B. "'Blood is subject to the laws of sacrilege,'the words of R. Meir. But R.
    Simeon and the sages say, '[Blood] is not subject to the laws of
    sacrilege.'"

C. What is the reason for saying [blood] is not subject to the laws of
    sacrilege?

D. Ulla said, "Scripture says, 'I have given it [the blood] to you   (Lev.
    17:11).' [This means that the blood] is yours [to use, and therefore is not
    subject to the laws of sacrilege]."

E. A student from the school of Ishmael taught [similarly], "Scripture says, 'I
    have given it to you] for making atonement' [meaning] I have given it [to
    you] for _atonement_, not to be subject to the laws of sacrilege."

F. R. Yohanan said, "Scripture said, 'For it is the blood that makes atonement
    through the life (Lev. 17:11)'; [this means that] the status of the blood
    before effecting atonement [i.e., before tossing it] is the same as the
    status of the blood after effecting atonement. Just as the laws of sacrilege
    do not apply to it after [it is tossed to effect] atonement, just so the laws
    of sacrilege do not apply to it before [it is tossed to effect] atonement."

G. But I might argue [the opposite, namely] just as the laws of sacrilege apply
    [to the blood] before [it is tossed to effect] atonement, just so do the
    laws of sacrilege apply after [it is tossed to effect] atonement.

H. [This last conclusion is absurd, however,] for can there ever be an item that
    is subject to the laws of sacrilege _after_ it has served its mandated purpose?
    [Certainly not! We are thus right ion rejecting G and accepting F.]

I. Why [do you say] there can be no such item?

J. [11B] Lo, [an example of just such an item is] the ash removed from the
    altar. This has served its mandated purpose, and yet it is subject to the
    law of sacrilege.

K. [We reject J's argument because ash removed from the altar cannot be used to
    derive other rules,] for the rule governing ash removed from the altar, and
    the [rule for] sacrificial portions of the scapegoat, [are found in] two
    [separate] Scriptural verses which [teach the] same rule. And whenever two
    Scriptural verses teach the same rule, they cannot be used to adduce [that
    same rule as regards anything else. Thus the objection raised by I-J has no
    basis.]

L. [We now respond to K. K's objection] works fine for one who [takes Scripture
    to say] that the scapegoat is not available for private use [and so falls
    under the same rule as the ash]. But what can you say to one [who interprets

[Scripture to] say that [the scapegoat] is available for personal use? [Now
the rule for the scapegoat is not like that for the ash.]

M. [The authority of K responds that the same argument can be made on the basis
of the ash and the holy garments of the priest,] for [the rule for] the ash
and [the rule for] the holy garment [are also found in] two [separate]
Scriptural verses which [teach the] same rule. And whenever two Scriptural
verses teach the same rule, they cannot be used [to adduce that same rule as
regards anything else].

N. [This restatement of K is subject to the same objection as before.] This
argument works fine for our rabbis, who hold [that Lev. 16:23, which says,
"Then Aaron shall come into the tent of meeting, and shall take off the linen
garment . . .] and shall leave it there," teaches [that these garments] do
not need to be buried, [and so remain subject to sacrilege, just like the
ashes]. But what can you say to R. Dosa, who ruled that it is permitted for
a common priest to use [such garments? On this view, they are not subject to
the laws of sacrilege, and so are not like the ash.]

O. [The authority of K responds that even so his argument is sound because it
can be made as well on the basis of the ash and the heifer the neck of which
is to be broken to atone for an anonymous murder (Deut. 21:1f),] for [the
rule for] the ash and the [rule for the] heifer the neck of which is to be
broken [are found in] two [separate] Scriptural verses which [teach the] same
rule. [And whenever two Scriptural verses teach the same rule, they can not
be used to adduce that same rule as regards anything else.]

P. [Once again we can reject this argument on the same grounds as before.] This
[claim of K's] is fine for one who says that no such [two separate verses of
Scripture] can be used to adduce [a rule as regards anything else]. But what
can you say to someone who says that [such verses] may be used to adduce
[rules as regards other things]?

Q. [The authority of K responds that he can make his case on the basis of these
verses even in light of P's objection.] For both verses [cited in O] point
to specific exemptions. The first verse says: "the heifer" and the second
"place it on the altar. The emphasis indicates that these [particular

things] are always subject to the laws of sacrilege, but other things are
not. [The end result of all this is that the claim of I stands unchallenged,
namely, that the altar ash is subject to the laws of sacrilege even though it
has fulfilled its function. This in turn bolsters G's claim that the laws of
sacrilege apply to the blood both before and after it has been tossed.]

II.

A. Drink offerings at the outset: the laws of sacrilege apply to them [but after
   they have gone forth to the pits, the laws of sacrilege do not apply]
   [M.3:3D]:

B. Let us say that this Mishnah-passage is not in agreement with R. Eleazar b.
   R. Sadoq, for it is taught that R. Eleazar b. R. Sadok says, "There was a
   small passageway between [the top of the altar-] ramp and the [surface of
   the] altar on the west side of the altar. Once every seventy years, the
   young priests would go down [into it] and bring up [masses of] congealed
   wine which were like fig-cakes, and would burn these in a sacred place.
   [This is to fulfill what Num. 28:7] says: 'You shall be sure to offer the
   libation-offering to God in holiness.' Now just as the offering is to be
   done in holiness, so too is its burning to be done in holiness." [That is,
   the libation-wine remains holy and so subject to the laws of sacrilege even
   after the offering is made, against the rule at M.]

C. On what basis does [Eleazar] draw this conclusion?

D. Said Rabina, "He reaches [this conclusion by drawing an analogy between the
   word] 'holiness' used here and the word 'holiness' used elsewhere. Here it
   is written ['You shall be sure to offer the libation] in holiness' and
   elsewhere (Ex. 29:34) it is written, 'You shall burn what remains [overnight]
   with fire. It is not to be eaten because it is [in a status of] holiness.'
   Now just as what remains overnight is burnt in a state of holiness, so too
   [libation wine left over after the offering] is deemed to be in a state of
   holiness."

E. You could even say that R. Eleazar b. R. Sadoq [holds that the wine remains
   holy only if it is caught] part way down, [but if it falls all the way to the
   bottom, it becomes unconsecrated as Mishnah says].

F. There are those who say "Let us say that [in fact] our Mishnah agrees with R. Eleazar b. R. Sadoq [in that wine caught] part way down [is still consecrated as Eleazar has said, and that it becomes unconsecrated only when it reaches the bottom of the pit]."

G. They say, "No, [Mishnah holds that leftover libation wine is unconsecrated in all cases. The claim that it remains holy if caught part way down] is [merely] a rabbinic enactment."

H. [How can this be called a rabbinic enactment since R. Eleazar proves it] with a citation from Scripture?

I. [His citation of Scripture is not a proof but serves merely as] support.

Mishnah claims that liability as regards sacrilege changes for both blood and for drink-offerings after these have been ritually used. The Gemara now challenges that assertion, as regards blood in unit I and as regards drink-offering in II. In both cases Gemara's challenge depends on Scriptural warrant. By successfully countering these challenges, the Gemara demonstrates that Mishnah's rules are in fact consistent with Scriptural law.

3:4A-F

A. The ashes [of the incense] of the inner altar and [of the wicks that remain] of the candelabrum--

B. are not available for benefit, but the laws of sacrilege do not apply.

C. He who sanctifies the ash to begin with--

D. the laws of sacrilege apply to it.

E. (1) Turtledoves which have not yet reached their maturity and (2) pigeons which have become superannuated

F. are not available for benefit, but the laws of sacrilege do not apply.

I.

A. It is clear [why ash] [12A] from the outer altar [must be placed in the ash-heap], for it is written [explicitly in Lev. 6:3,] "He shall place [the ash] near the altar."

B. But how do we know what the law is [regarding ash] from the inner altar?

C. R. Eleazar said, "[We know ash from the inner altar must be placed on the
    ash-heap] because Scripture says [in Lev. 1:16], 'You shall take away the
    crop with its feathers [and toss it next to the altar, on the east side where
    the ash goes].' Since [the ash mentioned here] cannot be from the outer
    altar, [which is discussed in Lev. 6:3,] we conclude that this is the ash
    from the inner altar."

D. [Eleazar's argument does not necessarily follow. What if] I say that this
    [verse, Lev. 1:16] and that [verse, Lev. 6:3] both refer to ash taken from
    the outer altar? [It is repeated twice, once to establish the requirement
    and once] to establish the place. [In this case, neither verse tells us
    anything about the disposition of ash from the inner altar].

E. [R. Eleazar responds,] "If this were so, Scripture could say simply 'next to
    the altar [on the east side].' Why does it go on to say, '[where] the ash
    goes'? It must be adding this phrase specifically to include] ash taken from
    [the other], inner, altar."

F. How do I know that this is true as well [for the burnt wicks] of the
    candelabrum?

G. [We know this because Scripture could simply have said "the place] of ash."
    [Since Scripture says "the place] of the ash," [adding an extra definite
    article, we conclude that other ash goes there too, namely, ash from the
    spent wicks of the candelabrum].

The Mishnah has given us rules for disposing of the ash and spent wicks
produced by the inner altar. The Gemara finds a Scriptural warrant for these
rules.

                              3:4G

G. R. Simeon says, "Turtledoves which have not yet reached their maturity--the
    laws of sacrilege do apply to them. Pigeons which have become superannuated
    are not available for benefit, and the laws of sacrilege do not apply."

I.

A. It make sense to assign this to R. Simeon, for he gives this same reasoning
   elsewhere, as it is taught, "R. Simeon says, 'If an animal will become fit
   [for the altar] after a certain time, but is dedicated [for holy use] before
   that time--lo [the one who uses it for personal benefit before it reaches
   age] transgresses a negative command [i.e. he commits an act of sacrilege.
   On the other hand, its slaughter is not deemed to be a proper act of
   sacrifice so that the one slaughtering it outside its proper place] is not
   liable to extirpation.'" [Cf. B. Hulin 81a]

B. But our rabbis [disagree. They do not see] how [birds] differ [from animals
   which are] too young. [For if one designates an underaged animal as an
   offering, that animal does not become consecrated. One who uses it does not
   thereby commit an act of sacrilege. This, rabbis say, should apply to
   underage birds as well.]

C. They say [in support of Simeon, "Animals and birds are different]. Underage
   [consecrated] animals are like animals which are blemished: they are
   redeemed [and other animals are brought in their stead. Since they are to be
   replaced, the one who uses them commits no sacrilege.] But it is taught as
   regards birds that since blemishes do not render them unfit (pasul), they are
   not redeemed. [Since they remain the property of the altar, the laws of
   sacrilege continue to apply.]"

II.

A. Said Ulla, "Said R. Yohanan, '[Animals which are] dedicated [to the altar and
   then] die, [their carcasses] are no longer subject to the laws of sacrilege,
   according to the word of Scripture.'"

B. When Ulla sat [in the session] and quoted this teaching, R. Hisda said to
   him, "Who would ever learn from you and from R. Yohanan your teacher? Where
   has the sanctity [that adhered to the animal] gone?"

C. [Ulla] said to him, "You could ask the same question of Mishnah itself [which
   says] Turtledoves which have not yet reached their maturity . . . and pigeons
   which have become superannuated are not available for benefit, but the laws
   of sacrilege do not apply [M. 3:4 E-F]." Here too we can ask what happened
   to the sanctity [that once adhered to the birds].

D. [Hisda] said to him, "[Your point is well taken]. I must concede that in
these cases the laws of sacrilege apply [to the dead animals or the
superannuated birds only] by rabbinic decree [and not by Scriptural law]."

E. [Yet this ruling in M. 3:4 poses] a difficulty for me [on other grounds. As
regards the first clause], can it be that something which is not subject to
the laws of sacrilege at the outset [such as the underaged turtledoves]
becomes subject to the laws of sacrilege later [upon maturing]?

F. [Ulla responds:] Why not? Lo, take the blood of the offering [for example].
At the beginning [of the sacrifice], the laws of sacrilege do not apply to
[the blood], but at the conclusion [of the sacrifice], the laws of sacrifice
do apply. For we have learned: The blood at the outset: the laws of
sacrilege do not apply to it. [When] it has gone forth to the Qidron Brook,
the laws of sacrilege do apply to it [M. 3:3B-C].

G. [Hisda dismisses this: But] I can say that even here the laws of sacrilege
apply at the outset [12B] for Rab said, "As to one who squeezes blood out of
a consecrated animal -- [the blood] is not available for benefit and the laws
of sacrilege apply to it." [There is still the problem, then, of finding a
precedent for Ulla's claim that something may be exempt from the laws of
sacrilege at the outset, and become subject to these laws later on.]

III.

A. [Turning to] the body [of this text]: Said R. Huna said Rab, "As to one
who squeezes blood out of a consecrated animal -- [the blood] is not
available for benefit and the laws of sacrilege apply to it."

B. R. Hamnuna responds [to Rab's ruling as follows]: "The milk of consecrated
animals and the eggs of [consecrated] turtledoves are not available for
benefit, but the laws of sacrilege do not apply to them. [It should follow
that the blood of such animals also is not subject to the laws of
sacrilege.]"

C. [R. Huna] said [in answer, " The blood is a distinct category. We apply [the
laws of sacrilege] to the blood because the sacrifice cannot occur without
blood, but we do not [apply the laws of sacrilege in the same way] to the
milk because the sacrifice can take place without milk."

D. R. Mesharshiyyah [finds material that is a necessary part of the animal, is
    unavailable for benefit and yet is not subject to the laws of sacrilege. He
    says], "Manure and excrement [from sacrificial animals] that are in the
    Temple courtyard are not available for benefit, but the laws of sacrilege do
    not apply, and money [paid if these are wrongly used] falls to the Temple
    treasury.

E. "Why [do I mention this]?

F. "Because no animal can exist without some excrement [in its bowels]." [It is
    a necessary part of the animal, just as the blood is. It follows that blood,
    like excrement, should not be subject to the laws of sacrilege.]

G. They [challenge Masharshiyyah's analogy] saying, "How can you make this
    comparison? It makes sense [to exempt the manure and] excrement [from the
    laws of sacrilege] because these come from the secular world: as soon as one
    [batch of food] passes through another is eaten. This is not so for blood,
    which is an intrinsic part of the body.

H. "[Further the ruling itself is contradictory], for it is taught [on Tannaitic
    authority], '[Manure and excrement . . .] are not available for benefit, but
    the laws of sacrilege do not apply, and money [paid if these are wrongly used
    falls to] the Temple treasury.' [Now if the laws of sacrilege do not apply,
    money paid for them should not become holy at all.]"

I. [Mesharshiyya responds: This ruling is not contradictory.] It in fact
    supports the view of Rabbi Eleazar, for said R. Eleazar, "As regards any item
    which the sages say is [partially] in a status of holiness and [partially]
    not in a status of holiness [such as the manure and excrement]—money [paid
    if it is wrongly used falls to] the Temple treasury."

Mishnah introduces a category of consecrated material which is not suitable
for the altar but which is nonetheless subject to sacrilege.   The example
provided by Mishnah 3:4G is a bird dedicated to the altar while still underage.
Unit I justifies Simeon's view that such an animal remains subject to the laws of
sacrifice even though it is not suitable for the altar. Hisda in II takes up an
implication of this ruling, namely that something not subject to the laws of

sacrilege when it is set aside (such as the underaged bird) could later become
subject (when the bird matures). The citation at IIG provokes the secondary
discussion in III.

3:5

A. The milk of animal-sacrifices and the eggs of turtledoves are not available
   for benefit, but the laws of sacrilege do not apply to them.

B. Under what circumstances?

C. In the case of what is made holy for the use of the altar. [The animal itself
   is dedicated to the altar. Since eggs and milk never serve as an offering,
   these do not become holy.]

D. But in the case of what is made holy for the upkeep of the Temple-house—

E. [If] one has sanctified a chicken, the laws of sacrilege apply to it and to
   its egg, [since it is the value of the animal as a whole that is being
   dedicated].

F. [If he sanctified] an ass, the laws of sacrilege apply to it and to its
   milk.

I.

A. Now what if one consecrates the value [of an animal] to the altar? Should
   not the laws of sacrilege apply [to its eggs or milk as well — just as if
   one dedicated its value to the upkeep of the Temple? And yet Mishnah's
   language seems to preclude this.]

B. Said R. Papa, "[This inference is correct]. The cited passage presents a
   lacuna and should read as follows: 'Under what circumstances? When one
   consecrates the body [of the animal] for the altar, but if one consecrates
   the value [of the animal] for the altar, it is as if one dedicated [the
   animal] for the upkeep of the Temple-house.

C. [Thus, for example,] if one consecrated a chicken [for the altar], the laws
   of sacrilege apply to it and to its eggs; [if one consecrated a] dam [for the
   altar], the laws of sacrilege apply to it and to its milk.'"

Talmud extends Mishnah's law to a case not explicitly addressed by Mishnah.

3:6

A. Whatever is appropriate for [use on] the altar [13A] but not for the upkeep
    of the house,

B. for the upkeep of the house and not for the altar,

C. not for the altar and not for the upkeep of the house—

D. the laws of sacrilege apply thereto.

E. How so?

F. [If] one sanctified (1) a hole full of water, (2) a dung-heap full of dung,
    (3) a dovecot full of pigeons, (4) a tree covered with fruit, (5) a field
    full of herbs—

G. the laws of sacrilege apply to them and to what is in them.

H. But if he sanctified (1) a hole, and afterward it filled with water, (2) a
    dung-heap, and afterward it was filled with dung, (3) a dovecot, and
    afterward it was filled with pigeons, (4) a tree and afterward it filled with
    fruit, (5) a field and afterward it was filled with herbs—

I. "the laws of sacrilege apply to them but the laws of sacrilege do not apply
    to what is in them" [M. adds: the words of R. Judah.]

J. R. Yose [M. has Simeon] says, "He who sanctifies a field and a tree—the laws
    of sacrilege apply to them and to what grows in them,

K. "for they are the offspring of that which has been consecrated."

L. The offspring of the tithe of cattle may not suck from [a beast that is]
    tithe [of cattle].

M. And others donate [their beasts] thus [on condition that, if the tithe of
    their cattle should be a female beast, its milk should not be deemed
    consecrated but should be available for its offspring].

N. The offspring of a consecrated beast should not suck from consecrated
    beasts.

O. And others donate their beasts thus.

P. Laborers should not eat of dried figs which have been consecrated.

Q. And so: A cow should not eat of vetches which have been consecrated.

I.

A. [M. 3:6L] teaches, the offspring of the tithe of cattle may not suck from [a
    beast that is] tithe [of cattle]:

B. What is the scriptural source for this rule?

C. Said R. Ahadboi bar Ami, "It is derived [by analogy] with the word 'passing,'
    [which is used in connection with firstborn in Ex. 13:12] and 'passing'
    [used in connection with tithe of cattle in Lev. 27:32]. Just as a firstborn
    is subject to the laws of sacrilege, so also is the milk of a beast that is
    tithe of cattle subject to the laws of sacrilege."

D. [The law as regards] milk of a beast dedicated [to the Temple] is derived in
    the same way [from the laws of the firstborn. Now, however, the analogy is
    based on the word] "its mother" used in connection with firstborn (Ex. 22:29)
    and "its mother" used in connection with dedicated animals (Lev. 22:27).

II.

A. [Turning to M. 3:6P] Laborers should not eat of [dried figs which have been
    consecrated]:

B. What is the reason for this ruling?

C. Said R. Ahadboi bar Ami, "[The ruling is based] on what Scripture says [in
    Deut. 25:4, namely], 'Do not muzzle the ox while it is threshing your grain.'
    [In this case,] 'your grain' [means grain] belonging to you, not [grain]
    belonging to the Temple. [That is, Scripture specifically mentions personal
    grain because one might by mistake allow an ox to eat of it. Temple grain is
    not mentioned because it is taken for granted that this may not be eaten.]"

III.

A. One who threshes ql'ylyn-wood in a field belonging to the Temple commits
    sacrilege.

B. [This cannot be! For] we require [that a plant be] harvested before the laws
    of sacrilege [apply. How then can you say he has committed sacrilege as
    regards the ql'ylyn-wood, which is still in the field?]

C. Said Rabina, "[The point is well taken. Therefore we must] conclude that
    the dust clinging to the plant is consecrated and that it is] against this
    dust that he commits sacrilege [and not the plant]."

Talmud locates Scriptural warrant for the rules of M. 3:6L (unit I), and M.
3:6P (unit II). Unit III is here because of II, which introduces the eating of
grain.

3:7

A.   [13B] [If] the roots of a privately owned tree come into consecrated ground,

B.   or those of a tree which is consecrated come into privately owned ground,

C.   they are not available for personal benefit, but they are not subject to the
      laws of sacrilege.

D.   A well which gushes forth from a field which is consecrated—[the water] is
      not available for enjoyment, but the laws of sacrilege do not apply.

E.   [If] it went outside of the field, they derive benefit from it.

F.   Water which is in a golden jar—

G.   is not available for benefit but is not subject to the laws of sacrilege.

H.   [If] one put it into a glass, the laws of sacrilege apply to it.

I.   The willow-branch [set beside the altar]

J.   is not available for benefit but is not subject to the law of sacrilege.

K.   R. Eleazar b R. Sadoq says, "The elders would derive benefit from them by
      using them in their lulabs."

I.

A.   Said Resh Laqish, "[As regards water in the golden jar = M. 3:7F–G], none of
      it is subject to the laws of sacrilege unless there were [exactly] three logs
      [of water. In this case, we assume that this water has been measured for use
      as libation] and so deem it subject to the laws of sacrilege."

B.   But does not the second clause [of the Mishnah-passage, i.e., M. 3:7H]
      teach, If one put it into a glass, the laws of sacrilege do apply to it?
      From this we must conclude that the first clause means that [the water in the
      golden jar] is not subject to the laws of sacrilege], even [if it measures
      exactly] three logs.

C.   [To account for the aforementioned Mishnah-passage, we must recast Resh
      Laqish's rule as follows.] If this were said [-- that the laws of sacrilege
      apply only to three logs of water --], it was said only as regards the second
      clause. [We should thus understand Resh Laqish as follows: "M. 3:7H says If
      one put it in a glass,] the laws of sacrilege apply to it. Said Resh
      Laqish, 'The laws of sacrilege do not apply unless [the glass] contains
      [exactly] three logs [of liquid].'"

D. [But this cannot be] for R. Yohanan said, "All [the water in the glass, i.e.
    regardless of amount] is subject to the laws of sacrilege." [Thus Resh
    Laqish's statement must be referring to the first clause, F–G, after all,
    meaning that the water is subject to sacrilege only if it measures 3 logs.]

II.

A. [We can challenge Resh Laqiah on other grounds.] Are we to conclude [from
    the above] that Resh Laqish deems [three logs of water] to be the fixed
    quantity [necessary for the libation]?

B. [Such a conclusion is impossible, for the following shows that Resh Laqish
    holds that there is no fixed quantity of water for the libation:] "Said R.
    Eleazar, 'If one performs the water-libation for the holiday of Booths on the
    holiday but outside of the Temple–Court, this one is liable [to extirpation,
    cf. Lev. 17:3f].'

C. "R. Yohanan in the name of Menahem of Yodapa said, '[We see here that] R.
    Eleazar accepts the interpretation of R. Aqiba, who explains [Scripture's use
    of the plural in] 'their libations [Num. 29:19]' to mean that wine-libations
    and water-libations are subject to the same laws. [Just as wine-libations
    must be performed in the Temple Court, so must water-libations].'

D. "Resh Laqish then said, 'Does this then mean that since wine-libations are to
    be three logs in quantity, water-libations also must be three logs in
    quantity?' [The implied answer is no, indicating] that Resh Laqish does not
    think there is a prescribed quantity of water."

E. [In fact, Resh Laqish does hold that three logs is a prescribed limit; C–D do
    not present a proper interpretation of Resh Laqish's ruling.] He is here
    simply pointing out the implication of Menahem of Yodapa's view. [Thus Resh
    Laqish's understanding of Mishnah still stands.]

    Resh Laqish in I.A offers an interpretation of Mishnah's rule.   The Gemara
shows that the critiques launched against Resh Laqish in I.B–D and II can not be
sustained.   The interpretation of I.A thus remains.

3:8A-F

A. A nest which is up at the top of a tree which has been consecrated

B. is not available for benefit, but is not subject to the laws of sacrilege.

C. And that which is on an asherah tree--

D. one may flick off with a reed.

E. One who sanctifies a forest--

F. the laws of sacrilege apply to the whole of it.

I.

A. [14A] [It has been stated on] Amoraic authority:

B. ["If an object used for] idolatrous worship fell apart by itself--R. Yohanan
    said, 'It is forbidden [for an Israelite to use the pieces],' but Resh Laqish
    said, 'It is permitted.'"

C. R. Yohanan said it is forbidden because [its status as an] idolatrous object
    has not been annulled.

D. Resh Laqish said it is permitted because [its status as an idolatrous object
    has been annulled, for its worshipper] surely says, "If it cannot rescue
    itself, how can it rescue me?" [He thus no longer regards it as worthy of
    worship and so it loses its idolatrous status.]

E. Resh Laqish responded to R. Yohanan, "[Mishnah proves its status is annulled,
    for Mishnah says in 3:8A]: A nest which is at the top of a consecrated tree
    is not available for benefit, but is not subject to the laws of sacrilege.
    And that which is on an asherah tree one may flick it with a reed. Now is it
    not the case that the [branches out of which the nest is made] were broken
    off [from the Asherah] itself? And yet Mishnah teaches one may flick it with
    a reed. [It follows that pieces broken off of an idolatrous object lose
    their idolatrous status.]"

F. [Yohanan replies,] "No! The twigs [out of which the nest is made] were
    brought from elsewhere [and not from the Asherah-tree, and so were never in
    the status of idolatrous objects]."

G. If so, why [does Mishnah] say, a nest in a tree which has been consecrated is
    not available for benefit, but not subject to the laws of sacrilege [M. 3:8A-

B]? [Does this not assume that a nest is made from materials derived from
the tree in which it is found?]

H. [No, Mishnah's rule] refers to growth that has become intertwined in the nest
after [it was built], and Mishnah reasons that [one should not derive benefit
from such growth, even though] it is not subject to the laws of sacrilege.
[The material of the nest proper is not deemed to be from the consecrated
tree, however.]

I. Here too [as regards the nest in the Asherah-tree] it makes sense to assume
that [some of the material comes from the tree in which the nest is found].
For otherwise, why should Mishnah say, You may flick it with a reed? Let him
simply take it! [Mishnah requires care in removing the nest because it is
deemed to contain material from the Asherah-tree.]

J. Said R. Abahu, "[In fact,] R. Yohanan said, '[Mishnah] always [assumes that
the nest material] comes from elsewhere [and not from the Asherah-tree].'
Why then say, You may flick it off? [Let him just take it.]

K. "[This rule means that] you are to flick the young birds off the nest [since
these are in a prohibited status. The rule does not refer to the nest.]"

L. Said R. Jacob to R. Jeremiah, "[We must reject K, for] these young birds are
in either case [i.e., whether from the consecrated tree or the asherah tree]
available for use. [There is no reason to rule that they must be flicked
off.] But their eggs in either case are prohibited [since the eggs depend on
the tree for survival." In his view, eating the eggs thus constitutes
deriving benefit from the tree.]

M. Said R. Ashi, "[The birds can be deemed taboo as well, for] if the young
birds require feeding [by the mother, then they depend on the tree and so]
are just like the eggs, [that is, in a prohibited status. It follows that
Mishnah must require them to be removed through flicking, but the nest itself
may be removed by hand, indicating it is of no concern.]

Mishnah states that a nest found in a consecrated tree may not be used for
benefit, but is not subject to the laws of sacrilege. It then turns to a nest
found in an Asherah-tree, that is, a tree used for idolatrous worship. This

nest, Mishnah says, may not be touched (it must be "flicked" off). At issue for
the Gemara is the status of this latter nest. Yohanan claims it is like the nest
of a consecrated tree, that is forbidden to Israelites to use. Resh Laqish
argues that such a nest is in fact available for use, and that Mishnah's rule
that it may not be touched applies for other reasons. His view is sustained.

                              3:8G-I

G. And the Temple treasurers who brought wood--

H. The laws of sacrilege apply to the wood.

I. But the laws of sacrilege do not apply to the chips and [they do]   not
    [apply] to the foliage.

I.

A. Said Samuel, "[Mishnah assumes that they construct Temple buildings out of
    consecrated wood. In fact, however,] they construct them out of ordinary
    wood, and afterwards they consecrate [what they had built].

B. "What is the reason [for waiting until the work is done to consecrate it?
    The reason is to make the coins available for wages. This works as follows:]
    Whoever donates coins [for the building] thereby consecrates them. As soon
    as the building is completed, the Temple-treasurer says, 'Let the coins be
    deconsecrated by transferring their status to the building.' The coins then
    become deconsecrated and may be given to the workers as their wage."

C. [14B] They respond, "[The procedure of A-B is not done. This is how they
    pay the workers:] What do they do with the leftover incense? They would
    separate out an amount equal in value to wages owed the workers. They then
    deconsecrate [that incense by transferring its holy status] to the workers'
    money and then give [the incense to the workers]. Later they turn around and
    buy back the incense [from the workers] with consecrated coins collected from
    the new levy. Now why [go through all this if they could simply] transfer
    [the coin's status of] consecration to a building? [It follows that the
    simple procedure described in A-B was not possible.]"

D. [We concede that the transaction described in C was once done, but not
    because Samuel's proposal is impossible. Rather, C was done because] there
    was no building [to which the money's status could be transferred].

E. [D's explanation can not be. There must have been a building because B]
    refers to the workers' wages.

F. [D means that] there was no [finished] building worth the equivalent amount
    of money.

G. [This should not have stood in the way of Simeon's procedure, for] did not
    Samuel himself say, "Dedicated money worth a maneh which is deconsecrated by
    coin worth a perutah is [deemed to be fully] deconsecrated"? [This means
    that one could have deconsecrated the money by transferring its status even
    to an unfinished building worth less than the coins.]

H. [Samuel responds: I said] this only [to validate a transaction] that had
    already been done, not [to validate such a transaction] to begin with.

I. Said R. Papa, [rejecting Simeon's explanation,] "This is [the real reason]
    why they build the buildings only out of unconsecrated materials: just as the
    Torah is not given over to ministering angles [lest they profane it]. For
    they reason what if [the workers] need to lie down and they do so on [the
    building material], it turns out that they committed a sacrilege. [To avoid
    this all the materials are left unconsecrated until the building is
    completed.]"

II.

A. We learned: And the Temple-Treasurers who brought wood--the laws of sacrilege
    apply to the wood. But the laws of sacrilege do not apply to the chips nor
    to the foliage [= M. 3:8G-I]:

B. Why should such wood be subject to sacrilege? [Let them do what they do with
    a building. That is] let them use unconsecrated wood, lest [the workers]
    need to lie down and lie on them and it turns out that they committed
    sacrilege. [They can then consecrate the wood when they are actually ready
    to use it on the altar.]

C. Said R. Papa, "[This would indeed work] for wood that is to be stored for use at some later date. But we learn in this Mishnah-passage about wood to be used that same day, [and so which must already be in a consecrated status]."

Mishnah's rule assumes that the materials purchased for Temple construction become consecrated as soon as they are purchased. They would thus be immediately subject to sacrilege. Unit I argues, to the contrary, that the materials were in fact not consecrated until they formed the finished product.   Unit II asks whether this same condition applies to wood brought as fuel for the altar fire. If so, this wood would not become liable to sacrilege until it was actually ready to be used.

4:1

A. [15A] Things consecrated for the altar join together with one another [for making up the requisite quantity—a perutah's worth—to be subject to] the laws of sacrilege,

B. and to impose liability on their account for transgression of the laws of refuse, remnant and uncleanness.

C. Things consecrated for the upkeep of the house join together with one another [in regard to sacrilege].

D. Things consecrated for the altar and things consecrated for the upkeep of the house join together [for making up the quantity to be subject to] the laws of sacrilege.

I.

A. We are now [forced] to ask [the following]: Since [Mishnah 4:1D] says, Things consecrated for the altar and things consecrated for the upkeep of the house—even though one is consecrated in itself and one has only its value consecrated, nonetheless it says—they join together [to make up the minimum quantity subject to] the laws of sacrilege, why must A-B specifically say that things dedicated to the altar join with other things dedicated to the altar? [Since dedicated items of different statuses join together, does it not follow that dedicated items of the same status join toether?]

B. [It is necessary to mention specifically items dedicated to the altar] because Mishnah goes on to say [that two items of this status also join together] to impose liability for transgression of the laws of refuse, remnant and uncleanness, which is not so for an item dedicated for the upkeep of the house [and an item dedicated to the altar. That is, items of these different statuses do not join together as regards the laws of refuse, etc.]

C. Because of this [difference, the fact that items dedicated to the altar do join together to make up the minimum volume for sacrilege is stated

-77-

specifically so as to distinguish items of this status from items of
different statuses].

II.

A. Said R. Yannai, "It is clear that one commits sacrilege only for [misusing
items consecrated for] the upkeep of the house and for [misusing] burnt-
offerings.

B. "What is the reason?

C. "Scripture says (Lev. 5:15), 'If any one commits a sacrilege against anything
consecrated to the Lord. . . .' This means the laws of sacrilege apply only
to items consecrated to for the Lord [such as burnt-offerings, which are
completely turned to smoke]; but [other sacrifices] consecrated to the altar
[are not subject to the laws of sacrilege because] part of them goes to the
priests or to the owners."

D. [Mishnah implies the exact opposite, however,] for we learned [in M. 4:1D:]
Things consecrated for the altar join together with one another [for making
up the requisite quantity to be subject to] the law of sacrilege. . . .
[This implies that various kinds of sacrifices are subject to the laws of
sacrilege, not just burnt-offerings.]

E. [Yannai can respond that this Mishnah-passage reflects] a rabbinic decree
[and not Scriptural law].

F. [We can also challenge Yannai's view on the basis of M. 1:1:] Most Holy
Things which one slaughtered in the south [side of the altar] --the laws of
sacrilege apply to them. [This means that sin-offerings, guilt-offerings and
public peace-offerings are also subject to the laws of sacrilege.]

G. [Yannai can respond that here too Mishnah reflects] a rabbinic decree [and
not Scriptural law].

H. [We can also challange Yannai's view on the basis of M. 5:1:] One who derives
benefit from a sin-offering while it is alive--does not commit a sacrilege
until he lowers its value. If it is dead, he commits sacrilege if he derives
any benefit at all. [This indicates again that sin-offerings, and not just
burnt-offerings, are subject to the laws of sacrilege.]

I. [Yannai can respond that this is also] a rabbinic decree!

J. [How can he say that this last rule is from the rabbis?] Does not Scripture
    say this very thing?

K. For has it not been taught [on Tannaitic authority]: Rabbi says, "[What does]
    'All the fat is the Lords (Lev. 3:16)' mean?" [It means] that the
    sacrificial parts of even Lesser Holy Things are subject to the laws of
    sacrilege [i.e., the laws of sacrilege apply to the dead bodies of
    consecrated animals].

L. [In fact, Yannai can say that this too is] a rabbinic decree.

M. [How can he say this since Rabbi, K,] cites a specific passage of Scripture?

N. [The answer is that the Scriptural citation is used] only as a prooftext [and
    not as a source of the rule];

O. for, lo, Ulla said R. Yohanan said, "Holy things which have died are exempt
    from the laws of sacrilege according to [the clear meaning of] Scripture."
    [The ruling in K is thus a rabbinic interpretation, not a pure Scriptural
    law.]

P. [We now show that the citation in O refers to offerings, and not merely to
    dedicated things.] To what [Holy Things does O refer]?

Q. Could I say that O refers to items dedicated to the upkeep of the Temple,
    even if these should die? [This can not be, however, since even the carcass
    of a dead animal has some value,]

R. for even if one dedicates [the value] of garbage for the upkeep of the
    Temple, would this not [have some value and so] be subject to the laws of
    sacrilege? [Of course it would! O must refer therefore to items dedicated
    to the altar. The point is that the laws of sacrilege do not apply to dead
    holy things. This is in line with Yannai who says that the laws of sacrilege
    apply only to items dedicated to the upkeep of the Temple and to burnt-
    offerings.]

S. But is it not the case that items dedicated to the altar remain subject to
    the laws of sacrilege [even after they die] according to Scripture? [Such
    dead animals are not suitable for the altar anymore, and yet are subject to
    the laws of sacrilege. This also stands in contradiction to Yannai.]

T. Actually what the school of Yannai meant to say [in A] was that the laws of
    sacrilege as regards items dedicated for the upkeep of the Temple [and for

burnt-offerings] are derived from Scripture, but the laws [of sacrilege] as
regards items dedicated to the altar are not [Scriptural, but are the result
of rabbinic enactments].

Mishnah assumes that consecrated items must be of a certain bulk before they
become subject to uncleanness, sacrilege and the like. Anything smaller is of no
consequence. Mishnah now tells us that diverse bits of consecrated items may
join together to create that minimum bulk. Gemara in unit I simply informs us as
to why Mishnah must state this in three distinct rules (A-B, C, D). The reason
is that items of different statuses join together for some laws and not for
others. Unit II is dedicated to Yannai's proposition that in all events the laws
of sacrilege apply only to items that belong totally to the Temple, such as
burnt-offerings and items dedicated to the upkeep of the House. The conclusion,
stated in T is that Yannai is right as regards Scriptural law, but that the
Rabbi's have extended the laws of sacrilege to other consecrated items.

4:2A-B

A. [15B] Five things in a burnt-offering ['wlh] join together [to form the
    requisite volume for liability to sacrilege]: (1) the meat, (2) the
    forbidden fat, (3) the fine flour, (4) the wine, and (5) the oil.

B. And six in the thank-offering [join together]: (1) the meat, (2) the
    forbidden fat, (3) the fine flour, (4) the wine, (5) the oil, and (6) the
    bread.

I.

A. R. Huna taught Raba, "[Only] five things ever ['wlm] join together [to form
    the requisite volume for liability to sacrilege]."

B. He said to him, "Did you say 'ever'? But Mishnah says as regards thank-
    offering, And six in the thank-offering [join together: (1) the meat, (2)
    the forbidden fat, (3) the fine flour, (4) the wine, (5) the oil, and (6) the
    bread]."

C. He said, "Read 'burnt-offering' ['wlh] instead of 'ever'" ['wlm] [so that
    Huna's statement is that of M. 4:2A]."

II.

A. We have learned that our rabbis taught as follows:

B. [The meat of] burnt-offerings and their sacrificial portions join together
    [to form the requisite volume] of an olive's bulk to render one liable [if
    one offers them] outside [the Temple compound], and to render one liable for
    violation of the laws of refuse, remnant, and uncleanness.

C. This refers to burnt-offerings, but not to peace-offerings.

D. This ruling makes sense as regards [burning portions of a burnt-offering]
    outside the Temple, for a burnt-offering is to be entirely burnt on the altar
    [so that all of it legitimately] joins together [to determine liability], but
    [the meat of] a peace-offering [is not entirely burnt on the altar so its
    meat] does not all join together to determine liability].

E. But as regards the law of refuse, remnant, and uncleanness [this ruling does
    not make sense]. For why should [the meat and sacrificial portions of]
    peace-offerings not join together to form the requisite volume. For have we
    not learned [in M. 4:3: All portions subject to the law of] remnant join
    together [to form the requisite volume for liability] and all [portions
    subject to the law of] refuse join together? [Since all parts of a peace-
    offering are subject to the laws of remnant, etc., they should all join
    together when determining liability to these laws.]

F. [This point is well taken.] Let us say, then, that the rule at A should read
    as follows: [the meat of] a burnt-offering and its sacrificial portions join
    together [to form the requisite volume] of an olive's bulk so that the blood
    may be tossed on its behalf. And since they join together for the blood to
    be tossed, so too [do they join together] to determine liability [to
    sacrilege], etc., [thus leaving out the issue of refuse, remnant and
    uncleanness].

G. Who teaches [this version of the law]?

H. It is R. Joshua;

I. for it is taught [on Tannaitic authority]: R. Joshua says, "As regards any of
    the sacrifices ordained in the Torah, if there remains an olive's bulk of its
    flesh or an olive's bulk of its fat, the blood is tossed. If there is a

half-olive's bulk of flesh and a half-olive's bulk of fat [these do not join

together] and the blood is not tossed. But as regards the burnt-offering,

even if there is only a half-olive's bulk of meat and a half-olive's bulk of

fat [these join together to form the requisite volume] and the blood is

tossed, because every part [of the burnt-offering] is burned. And as regards

the meal-offering, even if the whole is preserved, the blood is not tossed

[T. Zeb. 4:3]." [That is, bits of a burnt-offering join together, but not

bits of any other offering, as C has said.]

J. What does meal-offering have to do [with the discussion]?

K. Said R. Papa, "[It is relevant because we mean] a meal-offering brought as

part of the animal sacrifice."

I establishes the correct reading for M. 4:2A. It is that the various parts

of a burnt-offering join together to create the minimum volume necessary to

violate the laws of remnant, etc. II then asks whether or not this applies also

to peace-offerings. The question arises because while all of the parts of a

burnt-offering belong to the altar, this is not true for all of the parts of a

peace-offering, some of the meat of which goes to the priest and the donor.

4:2C-3B

C. (1) Heave-offering, and (2) heave-offering of tithe, and (3) heave-offering

of tithe of dema'i, and (4) dough-offering, and (5) first fruits join

together to impose a prohibition and to impose liability to the added fifth

on their account.

M. 4:2C-D

A. All forms of refuse join together.

B. All forms of remnant joint together.

M. 4:3A-B

I.

A. What is the reason [for allowing dough-offering and first fruits to join

together with heave-offering to create the requisite volume]?

B. [The reason is] that they are all called "heave-offering" [in Scripture]:

C. concerning dough-offering it is written, "From the first of the baker's pan you shall offer dough as a heave-offering (Nu.15:20)."

D. First fruit too is called heave-offering, for it is taught [that the expression], "The heave-offering of your hand [Deut. 12:17]" refers to first fruit.

E. Surely the rest [namely, heave-offering, heave-offering of the tithe and heave-offering of tithe of dema'i] require no [explanation for why they combine with heave-offering. Their very name indicates that they are a kind of heave-offering.]

Talmud finds a Scriptural basis for the law of M. 4:2C.

4:3C-D

C. All forms of carrion join together.

D. All forms of creeping things join together.

I.

A. Said Rab [16A], "They teach [this only as regards forming the requisite volume for conveying] uncleanness, [since all carcasses are unclean].

B. "But as regards [forming the requisite volume for prohibited] eating, [meat from] clean animals and [meat from] unclean animals are considered separately [i.e., they do not join together]."

C. Levi [disagrees,] saying, "They also join together even [to create the minimum volume for] eating."

D. R. Assi said, "[Meat from] clean animals and [meat from] unclean animals are considered separately [because each type of meat is prohibited for a different reason]."

E. Some say that [Assi] disagrees with Rab [holding that pieces of meat prohibit for different reasons never join together].

F. And some say they do not disagree [i.e., that Assi and Rab agree that prohibited meats join together for those purposes for which they share a

common prohibition. Thus meat from the carcass of a clean animal and meat
from the carcass of an prohibited animal join together for purposes of
uncleanness, both coming from a carcass, but not for purposes of prohibited
eating, since only one comes from a prohibited animal.]

G. These [authorities in F] respond [as follows to those who say that pieces of
meat prohibited for different reasons never join together]: "[The meat of a]
dead heifer [a permitted animal] and [the meat] of a living camel [a
prohibited animal] do not join together [to form the minimum volume for
prohibited eating. This is because each type of meat is prohibited for
completely different reasons.]

H. "[But would not Assi agree] that if both animals were dead, their carcasses
would join together [for purposes of uncleanness since the carcasses now
share a common prohbition, namely as sources of carcass-uncleanness]?"

I. [The authorities of E respond: "No, for] this would contradict R. Assi [as
presented in E, who holds that meat of clean animals and meat of unclean
animals never join together, since they are of different categories]."

J. [The authorities of F try a second argument: "But then I can say that [if one
takes a limb] from each animal while it is alive, these limbs do join
together [because Assi's rule applies only when both animals are dead. The
point then is that these limbs join together because they share one
prohibition in common -- a limb cut from a living animal -- even though in
other ways they are of distinct categories.]

K. "And who [argues that this is in fact the case]? R. Judah, for Judah said,
'The law prohibiting cutting of the limb of a living animal applies to
unclean animals [as well as it does to clean animals. Thus a limb cut from a
living clean animal and one cut from a living unclean animal will join
together.] But what if both are dead? Then their meat does not join
together [since one animal is of a prohibited category and the other is not]
[Cf. B Hullin 101b].'" [The point is that there is at least one scenario in
which pieces of meat of diverse categories do join together, contrary to Assi
in E.]

L. [The authorities of F continue to counter Assi in E as follows:] "If what you say is so, [i.e. that meat of a dead clean animal and meat of a dead unclean animal never join together,] then why [does the baraita in G] hasten to teach that "meat from a dead heifer and [meat from] a living camel do not join together", seeing that even if they are both dead the meat does not join together? [If the meat of a dead unclean animal can not join with the meat of a dead clean animal, even though both share a common prohibition, namely, as meat from a carcass, then it is surely the case that meat from a living animal and meat from a dead animal do not join together, since they have nothing in common. The fact that this point has to be mentioned explicitly implies that if both are dead, their meat <u>does</u> join together, in conflict with Assi in E.]

M. "Further, it is taught on Tannaitic authority: 'A half-olive's bulk [of meat from] a living heifer and a half-olive's bulk [of meat from] a dead camel do not join [to form an olive's bulk of prohibited food]. But a half-olive's bulk [of meat] from a heifer and half-olive's bulk [of meat] from a camel, whether alive or dead, do join together.'

N. "[Now if you take the second clause to mean that the meat joins together no matter what] the second clause would contradict the first clause. Therefore we must read [the second clause to say] that if both animals are dead [or both are alive], their meat joins together. [This, too, stands in contradiction to assi's view in E.]"

O. [The authorities of E retort:] R. Assi responds to you [as follows]: "This Tanna [M] supposes that one prohibition can apply [even though the meat is already prohibited] by another prohibition. [That is, he holds that we deem both pieces of meat to be under a common prohibition -- namely, as carcasses -- even though they came originally from animals that were of utterly different categories (one permitted and one prohibited). He then claims that this one common prohibition has legal effect despite the different original statuses of the animals so that the two pieces of meat join together. I hold, to the contrary, that since the two pieces of meat are from different categories of animals, they can never have a single prohibition in common, and so never can join together.]

II.

A. [16B] R. Judah said Rab said, "For eating an olive's bulk [or more] of creeping things one is flogged."

B. What is the reason [for setting an olive's-bulk as the requisite volume]?

C. Because "eating" is written thereof, [and for any transgression involving eating, the minimum size is an olive's-bulk].

D. But did not R. Yose the son of R. Hanina teach before R. Yohanan, "[Lev. 20:25 says,] 'So you should set apart the clean beasts from the unclean, the unclean bird from the clean. You should not draw abomination upon yourselves through beast or bird or anything with which the ground is alive, which I have set apart for you to treat as unclean.' Here Scripture opens by talking about eating and concludes by talking about uncleanness. [What are we to conclude from this?] Just as [the minimum quantity needed to transgress the laws of] uncleanness is a lentil's bulk, so too [the minimum amount needed to transgress the laws of] eating is a lentil's-bulk, [and not an olive's-bulk as claimed in A]."

E. [Upon hearing Yose's argument], R Yohanan praised him.

F. But this view [that the minimum size is a lentil's-bulk seems to] contradict the view of Rab [who holds the minimum size is an olive's-bulk].

G. There is no contradiction. The one, [Yose's minimum size of a lentil's-bulk, refers to eating] dead [creatures, which convey corpse-uncleanness], while the other, [Rab's minimum of an olive's-bulk, refers to eating] living [creatures which are designated as unfit for food].

H. Said Abayye to him, "[This compromise does not work,] for Rab bases his view on Mishnah, and Mishnah teaches, all forms of creeping things [the word 'all' implying that] even if the creeping things are dead [the minimum size is the same, namely an olive's bulk]."

I. Said R. Joseph to [Abayye], "The assertion [that Rab is basing himself on this Mishnah-passage] is yours [alone. In fact,] Rab is basing himself on another teaching."

III.

A. [For saying that the minimum size for transgressing the law is a lentil's-bulk,] R. Yohanan praised [Yose = II E].

B. They objected [to Yohanan accepting Yose's argument on the following
    grounds:] "As for a [complete] limb, there is no minium size [for
    transgressing the law]--even if [one eats] less than an olive's-bulk of
    carrion or [touches] less than a lentil's-bulk from an unclean creeping
    thing, [if it is an entire limb it renders him unclean]."

C. R. Yohanan said, "[This is true, but] one is not <u>flogged</u> for such
    [trangressions unless he has eaten or touched at least] an olive's-bulk, [and
    it is flogging that is under discussion]."

D. [This seems to contradict Yohanan's earlier acceptance of Yose, who claims in
    II.D that a lentil's bulk is the universal minimum size. This apparent
    contradiction is resolved as follows:] Said Raba, "[The first statement,
    that the universal minimum size as regards prohibited eating is a lentil's
    bulk, refers to those creeping things] singled out by Scripture [as not
    suitable for food. The later statement of Yohanan in C, that the minimum
    size for liability to flogging is an olive's bulk, refers to all other
    creeping things.]"

E. Said R. Adda bar Ahava to Raba, "If what you say is so, then we should make
    the same distinction between beasts singled out [by Scripture as unsuitable
    for food] and those not so singled out. [Since we do not make such a
    distinction, it follows that it should not be made as regards creeping things
    either, that is, there should be no differences in minimum size. Yohanan's
    contradiction still stands.]"

F. [17A] [Raba] says [in response], "When the Merciful one draws an analogy
    [between all categories of animals in Lev. 20:25, saying, 'You shall set
    apart the clean beast from the unclean, the unclean bird from the clean].
    You shall not draw abomination . . .' [this is meant to show that there is a
    universal minimum size for all these animals as regards the laws of
    uncleanness. The analogy does not function to establish a single minimum
    volume among these beasts as regards prohibited eating, however. Thus the
    distinction I claim Yohanan sees between different classes of creeping things
    is a valid distinction.]"

At issue is the meaning of Mishnah's brief rulings at C and D. There Mishnah
states that all forms of carrion join together to create the minimum volume one
must eat to violate the law against eating prohibited meat. Unit I asks whether
Mishnah means that such carrion joins together for all purposes, even if some of
it is prohibited on other grounds. That is, does carrion from a permitted animal
and carrion from a prohibited animal join together to create a single bulk of
prohibited meat beacuse both are carrion, or does the different character of the
meat mean that it joins together only as a source of carrion-uncleanness but not
for other purpose? Having determined that the meat joins together only for
purposes of carrion-uncleanness, Mishnah proceeds in unit II, and its supplement
at III, to ask about the minimum volume Mishnah has in mind.

4:3E-G

E. The blood of a creeping thing and its flesh join together.

F. A general principle did R. Joshua state, "All things that are alike in the
    [duration of] uncleanness of each and in the requisite measure of each join
    together.

G. "[If they are alike] (1) in [duration of] uncleanness but not in requisite
    measure, (2) in requisite measure but not in [duration of] uncleanness, (3)
    neither in [duration of] uncleanness nor in requisite meaasure, they do not
    join together [to form the volume that is necessary to convey uncleanness]."

I.

A. Said R. Hanina said R. Zeira, thus also did R. Yose b. R. Hanina say, "[When
    Lev. 11:31 says,] 'These are the unclean things . . .' [it means] to teach
    that [material from all creeping things] joins together—even [flesh from
    one] creeping thing with [flesh from another] creeping thing, or [flesh from
    one] creeping thing with blood [of another], whether these are of the same
    species or from two [different] species."

B. [This might seem to contradict the ruling of M. 4:3F-G which says that items
    of different categories do not join together.] Said R. Joseph, however,

"There is no problem. The one ruling [that of R. Hanina] deals with [the
flesh or blood] of complete [animals, which are virulent in themselves.
These may combine to produce the requisite volume.] The other rule [that of
M. 4:3F-G] deals with [the flesh or blood] of parts of diverse animals.
[These parts are not virulent in themselves, and so can not combine with
items of different categories to create the minimum volume needed to convey
uncleanness.]"

C. On what basis do you say [that we make such a distinction between the flesh
   or blood of a whole animal and the flesh or blood of part of an animal]?

D. Because it is taught, "If [the requisite amount of blood from a dead thing]
   was poured out on the pavement, and its place was an incline and one
   overshadowed part of it, he is clean; if he overshadowed all he is unclean
   [Cf. M. Ohalot 3:3]."

E. Now what does "part of it" mean? I might say it means [that I overshadow]
   only a portion [of the requisite volume].

F. But lo, R. Hanina said Rabbi said, "If one has a quarter-log of blood [the
   requisite amount to convey uncleanness] and stirs it, this one remains pure."
   [Why? Since the requisite volume for conveying uncleanness is present, it
   must be because the blood is not from a complete animal.]

G. Do we not learn from this that we make a distinction between blood from a
   complete [animal in which case a quarter-log of blood conveys uncleanness]
   and blood from [only] a portion [of an animal, which blood does not convey
   uncleanness]?

II.

A. R. Matya b. Heresh asked R. Simeon b. Yohai in the Metropolis [Rome], "From
   where [do we know] that the blood of creeping things conveys uncleanness?"

B. He said to him, "[We derive this from Lev. 11:29], where Scripture says,
   'This is what is unclean for you. . . .' [There follows a list of creeping
   things and the phrase, 'these are unclean for you.' Since the second phrase
   clearly refers to the bodies of the creeping things, the first phrase must
   refer to the blood.]"

C. His students [impressed by this answer] said, "The son of Yohai has grown
   wise!"

D. He [Simeon] said to them, "[I did not come up with this on my own.] It is an
   established teaching from R. Eleazar bar R. Yose.

E. [This is how he came to learn it.] For once the authorities decreed that
   [Jews] should no longer observe the Sabbath, should not circumcise their
   sons, and should have intercourse with menstruant women [thus rendering
   themselves impure].

F. Upon hearing this R. Reuben ben Istroboli had his hair cut [in the Roman
   fashion] and sat among [the Romans without being recognized as a Jew].

G. He said, "Does one wish that one's enemy becomes rich or grows poor?"

H. They replied, "That he grow poor!"

I. He said, "If so, let [the Jews] not do work on the Sabbath so that they might
   grow poorer."

J. They said, "You have spoken well." And they annulled the decree.

K. He said further, "Does one want one's enemy to be weak or healthy?"

L. They said, "to be weak!"

M. He said, "If so let [the Jews] circumcise their sons on the eighth day so
   that they will become weak."

N. They said, "You have spoken well." And they annulled the decree [against
   circumcision].

O. He said further, "Does one want one's enemies to increase or decrease?"

P. They said, "To decrease!"

Q. He said, "If so, let [the Jews] refrain from sexual intercourse with
   menstruant women."

R. They said, "You have spoken well." And they annulled the decree [requiring
   intercourse with menstruant women].

S. When they discovered he was a Jew, they reinstituted [all the decrees.
   Thereupon the Jewish leaders] said, "Who should go [to Rome] and get the
   decrees annulled?"

T. [17B] [Someone replied,] "Let R. Simeon bar Yohai go for he has experience in
   miracles."

U. "And who shall go with him?"

V. "Let R. Eleazar b. R. Yose go!"

W. Said to them R. Yose, "Were my father Halafta still alive, could you say to him, 'Send your son to death'? [Of course not. Now, then, can you ask my son to go on such a mission?]"

X. Said to them R. Simeon [bar Yohai], "Were my father Yohai still alive, could you say to him, 'Send your son to death?' [Of course not, but I am still willing to go!]"

Y. Said to them R. Yose, "I myself shall go along so should R. Simeon [try to] punish [my son], I can protect him."

Z. [R. Simeon thereupon] pledged that he would not harm [the child].

AA. Nonetheless, he did do him harm.

BB. [It occurred as follows:] While they were on the road, this question was put to them: "From where do we know that the blood of creeping things is unclean?" R. Eleazar b. R. Yose blurted out, "[From Lev. 11:29, which says,] 'This is unclean for you.'" Said to him R. Simeon, "Your outburst shows you to be a brilliant scholar. [Nonetheless, because of your impatience,] the son [i.e., Eleazar] shall not return to the father." [It is from this outburst that Simeon learned the Scriptural exegesis he cites in B. Although the point of the story has now been made, Gemara continues its narration.]

CC. [Subsequently,] ben Tamalion [an evil demon] appeared and said, "If it is your pleasure, I shall go with you."

DD. Thereupon R. Simeon wept and said, "[Even] a maid of my ancestors' household [i.e., Hagar] was visited by [a good] angel three times, but I [am not visited by a good angel] even once. Nonetheless let some miracle occur [so that we are successful in Rome]."

EE. [In the meantime,] ben Tamalion went ahead and entered the emperor's daughter. When [Simeon] arrived, he said, "Out, ben Tamalion! Out, ben Tamalion"! and as he called out [ben Tamalion] left her [and she was cured]. The emperor said [to Simeon and Eleazar], "Ask what you will [and it shall be granted]," and he brought them into the storehouse to take whatever they wanted. There they found [a copy of] the decree [under discussion] and they took it and tore it up.

FF. It was this [visit that] R. Eleazar bar R. Yose [had in mind when he] said,
"While in Rome [in the royal storehouse] I saw [the Temple veil] and it was
splattered with blood."

Under consideration here is the same issue as puzzled Gemara's authorities
earlier, namely, whether or not items of diverse sorts can combine to create the
minimum quantity needed to convey uncleanness. Mishnah 4:3 says that items can
so combine only if they are of the same category. Hanina in I.A argues the
opposite. The remainder of Unit I resolves this apparanet conflict. This concern
with the blood's ability to convey uncleanness provides an excuse for the
discussion in II. Simeon's statement in D calls forth the long story in E-FF,
which explains in BB how Simeon learned this teaching.

                                   4:4A-E

A. Refuse and remnant do not join together, because they are of two [different]
    categories.
B. The creeping thing and carrion,
C. and so too, carrion and the flesh of a corpse—
D. do not join together with one another to impart uncleanness,
E. even in accord with the lesser of the two of them.

I.

A. Said R. Judah said Samuel, "[The authorities of Mishnah] taught [that refuse
    and remnant do not join together] only as far as conveying uncleanness to the
    hands is concerned, because [the uncleanness of hands is a matter] of
    rabbinic decree. But as regards the minimum requisite volume for prohibited
    eating, these do join together [since this prohibition is directly from
    Torah]."
B. For it has been taught [on Tannaitic authority]:

C. R. Eliezer says, "[Exodus 29:34 says,] 'It is not to be eaten for it is holy
    . . .' With this Scripture establishes a prohibition against eating any holy
    thing that is disqualified, [regardless of why it is disqualified. From this
    we learn that even refuse and remnant join together to create the requisite
    minimum volume for prohibited eating].

Samuel   limits the application of Mishnah's rule on the basis of a Scriptural
verse.

                                   4:4F—4:5

F. Food which has been made unclean by a Father of uncleanness and that which
    has been made unclean by an offspring of uncleanness join together to impart
    uncleanness in accord with the lesser remove of uncleanness of the two of
    them.

                                     4:4F

A. All foodstuffs join together—

B. to render the body invalid, at a volume of half a half-loaf of bread;

C. in the case of food, two meals for an 'erub [M. Erub. 8:2];

D. in the volume of an olive's bulk to impart uncleanness as food,

E. in the volume of a fig's bulk in connection with removal [from one domain to
    another on] the Sabbath [M. Shab. 7:4],

F. and in the volume of a date's bulk [for the volume prohibited for eating] on
    the Day of Atonement [M. Yoma 8:2].

G. All liquids join together—

H. to render the body invalid, at a volume of a quarter-log;

I. and for the mouthful [which it is forbidden to drink] on the Day of
    Atonement.

                                   M. 4:5

I.

A. It has been taught [on Tannaitic authority]:

B. R. Simeon says, "What is the reason [that food in the first degree of
    uncleanness joins together with food in the second degree of uncleanness]?"

C. The reason is that food in the second degree of uncleanness might possibly
    become unclean in the first degree [T. Toh. 1:1B].

D. But can food in the second degree of uncleanness become unclean in the first
    degree? [No!] This is impossible.

E. Said Raba, "This is what [Simeon] meant: What causes food to become unclean
    in the second degree if not food unclean in the first degree? [Since the one
    is the cause of the other, we deem them to be in the same category as regards
    joining together.]"

F. R. Ashi said, "[They should both then join with food unclean in the third
    degree, for] from the point of view of the third degree of uncleanness, food
    in the first degree of uncleanness and food in the second degree of
    uncleanness are both members of the same category [that is both are sources
    of uncleanness]."

M. 4:4F has food of different levels of uncleanness join together to create
the requisite volume to impart uncleanness. Talmud explains the logic behind
this ruling.

4:6A-B

A. [18A] 'Orlah--fruit and diverse kinds of the vineyard join together.

B. R. Simeon says, "They do not join together."

I.

A. Why does R. Simeon need [to be concerned] about joining together at all? Is
    it not taught, "R. Simeon says, 'Eating any amount [of forbidden food
    whatsoever renders one liable] to flogging'"?

B. [Rather, you should read R. Simeon's statement to] say, "They do not <u>need</u> to join them together [since one is liable for the eating of any amount]."

Talmud revises the tradition regarding Simeon's view in M. 4:6B in light of another of his teachings.

4:6C-D

C. Cloth and sacking, sacking and leather, leather and matting join together with one another [to form the requisite volume to receive uncleanness].

D. R. Simeon says, "That is because they are suitable to be made unclean as that which is used for sitting [with moshab-uncleanness]."

<u>I</u>.

A. A Tanna [gives the following illustration of how Mishnah's law might apply]: "If one takes a bit of each of the three [i.e. cloth, sacking and matting] and makes of them a [single] cloth to lie upon [and it is at least] three [handbreadths on each side]; or to sit upon [and it is at least] one [handbreadth on each side]; or as a holder and it is any size, [then it is susceptible to uncleanness]."

B. Why is a holder [susceptible at any size whatsoever]?

C. Said Resh Laqish said R. Yannai, "[It is susceptible at any size] because [even a small scrap] is of use to the weaver [for smoothing his threads, for example]."

D. A Tanaitic teaching says, "[It is susceptible at any size] because [even a small scrap] is suitable for fig-reapers [to use to protect their fingers]."

Gemara illustrates the application of Mishnah's ruling.

CHAPTER SIX

BAVLI MEILAH CHAPTER FIVE

5:1

A. "He who derives benefit to the extent of a perutah's value from that which is consecrated,

B. "even though he did not cause deterioration [through use of it],

C. "has committed an act of sacrilege, "the words of R. Aqiba.

D. And sages say, "Anything which is subject to deterioration through use--he has not committed an act of sacrilege unless he caused deterioration through use,

E. "but anything which is not subject to deterioration through use--once he has derived benefit from it, he has committed an act of sacrilege."

F. How so?

G. [If a woman] put a chain around her neck,

H. a ring on her finger,

I. drank from the cup of gold [used for water for the animal to be offered as the whole-offering of the day],

J. once she has derived benefit from it, she has committed an act of sacrilege.

K. [If a man] put on a shirt,

L. covered himself with a cloak,

M. used an axe to split wood--

N. he has not committed sacrilege unless he has caused deterioration through use.

O. [If] one derives benefit from a sin-offering [lamb] when it was alive, he has committed an act of sacrilege only if he has caused deterioration.

P. But if this was after it was dead, once he has made use of it, he has committed an act of sacrilege.

I.

A. [A Tannaitic authority] taught:

B. R. Aqiba concedes to sages in respect to things which are subject to
    deterioration [that if one derives benefit but does not cause deterioration,
    he has not committed an act of sacrilege] [T. 2:1].

C. About what do they disagree?

D. Said Raba, "[They disagree about what is not subject to deterioration through
    use; for example,] a garment worn between [other garments] or [a garment made
    of] thick cloth." [These suffer no perceptible deterioration through being
    used. Aqiba holds that since these are used at all, the wearer has committed
    sacrilege. Sages hold that since their is no measuarble deterioration their
    use does not constitute sacrilege.]

E. Our rabbis taught [in support of sages, "Lev. 5:15 says], 'If any one . . .'-
    -whether a commoner, a prince or an anointed priest --'commits a sacrilege'--
    a sacrilege is anything that causes a change [in the physical character of a
    holy item. If no physical change is apparent, no sacrilege has occurred.]"

F. Aong these same lines, (Nu. 5:12) says, "If any man's wife goes astray and
    changes (m'lh bwm'l) [partners] against him."

G. And (1 Chr. 5:25) says, "But they changed [wym'lw] from the [18B] God of
    their fathers and went after the baals." [These verses prove that
    perceptible change must occur for the laws of sacrilege to apply.]

II.

A. One might [wrongly assume that sacrilege occurs only if] one causes
    deterioration, but derives no benefit; or derives benefit but causes no
    deterioration,

B. or that it applies only to what is attached to the ground;

C. [or that one can be guilty of sacrilege through the act] of an agent [even if
    the agent is] not carrying out his commission.

D. [To eliminate these possibilities,] Scripture says, "[If anyone commits a
    sacrilege] and sins. . . ." (Lev. 5:15).

E. The words "and sins" is used [in Lev. 22:9] in connection with heave-offering
    and here (Lev. 5:15) in connection with sacrilege. Just as the "sin"

mentioned in connection with heave-offering consists of causing deterioration
and deriving benefit, and the one who causes the deterioration derives the
benefit [therefrom], and the thing in which he caused the deterioration is
also the thing from which he derived benefit, and his causing deterioration
and deriving benefit result from the same act, and it is something separated
from the soil, and can be the result of an agent carrying out his commission-
-so also the "sin" mentioned in connection with sacrilege consists of causing
deterioration and deriving benefit, and the one who causes the deterioration
derives the benefit, and the thing in which he caused the deterioration is
also the thing from which he derived benefit, and his causing deterioration
and deriving benefit result from the same act, and it is something separated
from the soil, and can be the result of an agent carrying out his commision.

F.   [At this point] I know only that sacrilege applies to items I can eat and
     from which I can derive benefit. From where do I know [that sacrilege
     applies even to] items that do not suffer deterioration?

G.   And from where [in Scripture] do I know that if one eats of it and one's
     fellow eats of it, or if one derives benefit from it and one's fellow derives
     benefit from it, or one derives benefit from it and one's fellow eats of it
     or if one eats of it and one's fellow derives benefit from it that all these
     join together [to form the minimum volume for sacrilege] even if [this]
     occurs only over a long period of time?

H.   [We adduce all this] from [Lev. 5:15], which says, "commits a sacrilege" --
     meaning [sacrilege is commited] in all these ways.

I.   However [Scripture seems to indicate exactly the opposite], for just as the
     word "sin" used on conjunction with heave-offering (Lev. 22:9) concerns a
     case in which two separate acts of eating [or deriving benefit] do not join
     together to create the minimum volume [for prohibited eating], so when the
     word "sin" is used in conjunction with sacrilege, it should mean that two
     such acts do not join together.

J.   From where [in Scripture] do we know [that foods join together to form the
     requisite volume] even if he ate some today and some tomorrow or even if
     there is a longer time [between the two occasions of eating]?

K. From [Lev. 5:15] which says, "commits a sacrilege" -- meaning in all these
    ways.

L. However [Scripture seems to indicate exactly the opposite], for   just as
    the word "sin" is used in connection with heave-offering, for which
    deterioration and benefit must occur together, [so when the word "sin" is
    used in conjunction with sacrilege, it should mean that deterioration and
    benefit must occur together].

M. From where [in Scripture] do we know that food one eats and food one's fellow
    eats join together, even if [these eatings are separated by as much as] three
    years?

N. From [Lev. 5:15] which says, "commits a sacrilege" -- meaning in all these
    ways.

O. However [Scripture seems to indicate exactly the opposite], for just as the
    word "sin" is used in connection with heave-offering, [for which the
    requisite volume is achieved at any time] [19A] until it leaves its holy
    status for a secular status, [so when the word "sin" is used in connection
    with sacrilege, it means that the requisite volume can be made up over any
    length of time].

P. [We now turn to a different line of inquiry entirely. We have just seen that
    if a consecrated item is used for secular purposes, an act of sacrilege is
    committed. But what if a consecrated item is transferred] from one holy
    status to another--such as if one brought a bird-offering for a man suffering
    from a flux, or for a woman suffering from a flux or for a woman after
    childbirth, and then paid the Temple-tax with it; or if he brought a sin-
    offering or a guilt-offering from items dedicated to the Temple? [Does its
    use as another kind of consecrated item consitute an act of sacrilege as
    regards its original status?]

Q. "He commits sacrilege with it as soon as he changes its status," the words
    of R. Simeon. R. Judah says, "He does not commit sacrilege with it] until he
    tosses its blood [in the name of the second offering, thus rendering the
    change in status irreversible]."

R. From where [in Scripture do we find support R. Simeon's view]?

S. From [Lev. 5:15,] which says, "commits a sacrilege" -- meaning in all these
    ways.

III.

A. [Returning to the first comment:] the Master said, "[When Lev. 5:15 says,]
    'If anyone [commits a sacrilege. . .]' the meaning is [whether the person is]
    a commoner, a prince or an anointed priest."

B. What else might one think? It is obvious [that commoners, princes and
    anointed priests are included since Scripture clearly] says "anyone."

C. [It is necessary to say this for otherwise you might think the priests are
    excluded.] For you might say that since the Merciful one says, "Whoever puts
    any of it [the anointing oil] on a stranger [i.e., non-priest]," we might
    conclude that since [the priest] is not a stranger and is anointed with that
    oil, [he falls into a unique category]. Hence [the explicit mention of
    priest is necessary] to teach us [that even the priest can commit
    sacrilege].

IV.

A. The Merciful One draws an analogy between [the laws of sacrilege] and the
    laws of the suspected wife [as regards consecrated things that are not
    subject to deterioration through use, between the laws of sacrilege] and the
    laws of idolatry [as reagrds consecrated things that are subject to
    deterioration through use], and [between the laws of sacrilege] and the laws
    of heave-offering [as regards consecrated things that are edible].

B. [The analogy between sacrilege and] the suspected wife: [just as the
    suspected wife commits a transgression by having illicit relations with
    another] even if she suffers no physical deterioration, so too is the case
    with consecrated items [which are not subject to deterioration through use.
    In this case, an act of sacrilege is committed as soon as someone derives
    personal benefit from it, the view of sages in M. 5:1E.] Thus if one puts a
    [consecrated] ring on [her finger,] she has [straightaway] commited an act
    of sacrilege.

C. The Merciful One draws an analogy [between sacrilege] and idolatry [as
    follows: the laws of idolatry do not apply] until the object in question has

undergone a physical change. The same is true of the use of consecrated
items [which are subject to deterioration through use. Sacrilege is committed
through the use of such an items only when physical deterioration is
apparent, the view of sages in M. 5:1D. Thus, one does not commit sacrilege
by using a consecrated axe] until he is chopping with that ax and damages it
[M. 5:1 M-N].

D. The Merciful One draws an analogy between sacrilege and the laws of heave-
offering [as follows]: [Lev. 22:14 says,] "If one has eaten [of a holy thing
unintentionally, he must repay its value plus an added fifth to the priest]."
This excludes [from punishment] one who damages [but does not eat] the heave-
offering. The same is true for any consecrated item that can be eaten, that
is, when one damages it [but does not eat it], he has not committed a
sacrilege.

V.

A. [Turning to Mishnah's example of items that do not deteriorate:] How so? If
a woman put a chain around her neck [M. 5:1F-G]:

B. Said R. Kahana to R. Zabed, "[This example is inapplicable, for] is not gold
susceptible to deterioration? Take [for example] the gold [jewelry] of the
daughter-in-law of Nun [a rich man. The jewelry he gave to his daughter was
found to have lost weight over time.] Where did [the lost gold] go [if it
was not lost through normal wear]?"

C. [R. Zabed] said to him, "Perhaps the gold [jewelry] was like that which your
daughter-in-law used to throw around. [That is, perhaps it did not
deteriorate through normal wear but was damaged through misuse.]

D. "Besides [you must admit] that this is not a case in which one derives
benefit from the item and simultaneously causes the deterioration. [That is,
the deterioration occurs only gradually.]"

E. [R. Kahana responds, "Nonetheless] is there not always some deterioration
[that results from wearing jewelry]?"

VI.

A. [Turning to M. 5:1/O:] If one derived benefit from a sin-offering when it was
alive, he has committed an act of sacrilege only if he has caused
deterioration:

B. When [does such deterioration make a difference]? If we are dealing with an
    unblemished animal—lo, it is like a golden cup [in which deterioration
    through use is insignificant and does not effect its use].

C. Said R. Papa, "We are dealing with a blemished animal. [Such a consecrated
    animal must be sold. Any deterioration it suffers will lower the price it
    will fetch.]"

Aqiba and sages disagree in Mishnah as to what constitutes the commission of
sacrilege.   Aqiba   holds that   the mere use   of a consecrated   item for personal
benefit is sufficient. Sages   claim that if   the consecrated object   can suffer
deterioration   through   use, then   such deterioration must   have taken place   for
sacrilege to occur.   Unit I finds Scriptural warrant for sages' view.   II-IV
spell out the criteria for sacrilege more fully.   Unit II, with its gloss at III,
is little more than a lengthy exegesis of Leviticus 5:15.   IV links the laws
regarding the definition of sacrilege to other, parallel rulings.   Having laid
out the general principles in line with M. 5:1 A-E, Talmud in V and VI turns to
an examination of the specific examples supplied in M. 5:1F-G and O.

5:2-3

A. [19B] [If] one derived benefit to the extent of a half-perutah and caused
    deterioration to the extent of a half-perutah,

B. or [if] he derived benefit to the extent of a perutah from one thing and
    caused deterioration to the extent of a perutah in some other thing—

C. lo, this one has not committed an act of sacrilege—

D. until he will derive benefit to the extent of a perutah and [/or] cause
    deterioration to the extent of a perutah in the very same thing.

M. 5:2

A. One does not commit sacrilege after another has committed sacrilege [in the
    same thing] in the case of consecrated things,

B. except for a beast or a utensil of service.

C. How so?

D. [If] he rode on a beast and his fellow came along and rode on it, and yet
    another came and rode on it--[B. adds: all of them have commited sacrilege;]

E. drank from the golden cup [M. 5:1I] and his fellow came along and drank from
    it, and yet a third party came along and drank from it--[B. adds: all of
    them have commited sacrilege;]

F. pulled wool out of a sin-offering, and his fellow came along and pulled wool
    from the sin-offering, and yet a third came along and pulled wool from the
    same sin-offering--

G. all of them have committed an act of sacrilege.

H. Rabbi says, "Anything which is not subject to redemption is subject to a case
    of sacrilege following sacrilege.

M. 5:3

I.

A. Whose view does our Mishnah [M. 5:3 A-B, follow]?

B. R. Nehemiah.

C. For it is taught [on Tannaitic authority]: "One does not commit sacrilege
    after another has committed sacrilege [with the same thing] except for a
    beast alone: R. Nehemiah says: '[One may do so] with beast or with a vessel
    of service' [T. 2:6]."

D. What is the reason for the first rule [in the tradition cited above which
    excludes beasts alone]?

E. [They are excluded because] the role of the beast is [explicitly] mentioned
    in Scripture, as it is written [Lev. 5:16, "The priest makes atonement for
    him through] the ram of the guilt-offering." [Since beasts are specifically
    mentioned as crucial to the ritual, they are subject to sacrilege after
    sacrilege.]

F. R. Nehemiah replies to you, "It is an argument a fortiori [that utensils of
    service should likewise be excluded, that is, susceptible to sacrilege after
    sacrilege] for since they cause other things [put into them] to become holy
    [and so susceptible to sacrilege after sacrilege], should they not themselves
    surely [be susceptible to sacrilege after sacrilege]?"

II.

A. [Turning to Mish. 5:3H: <u>Rabbi says, "Anything which is not subject to</u>
    <u>redemption is subject to a case of sacrilege following sacrilege"</u>:

B. Lo, this agrees exactly with the first statement [i.e., M. 5:3A-B which
    exempts from the laws of sacrilege everything which is subject to redemption.
    Why repeat this same relationship in a second way?]

C. Said Raba, "[It is repeated because Nehemiah (in M. 5:3A-B) and Rabbi (in M.
    5:3H)] in fact do disagree about something, namely firewood [brought for the
    altar].

D. "For our rabbis taught 'One who says: I take it upon myself to bring
    firewood to the Temple may not bring less than two logs [but need bring
    nothing else].' Rabbi says, 'The firewood is like an offering and so must
    have a salt-offering and a wave-offering [brought with it as well.' Since,
    in Rabbi's view, the wood is like a beast, it is also subject to sacrilege
    following sacrilege. On the other hand, since M. 5:3A-B holds that the wood
    is not like a sacrifice, it follows that its is not subject to sacrilege
    after sacrilege.]"

E. Said Raba, "[Rabbi's view makes no sense, for] according to Rabbi's view
    [bringing] firewood [for the altar], would require one [to bring more]
    firewood [just as is the case for bringing any sacrificial beast]."

F. And R. Papa said, "[Rabbi's view makes no sense, for] according to Rabbi's
    view [bringing] firewood [for the altar], would require one [to bring] a
    handful [of meal-offering just as is the case for bringing any sacrificial
    beast]."

G. [On the basis of E and F, then, we must reject C's rational for why the rule
    of of Mishnah 5:3A-B is apparently repeated at M. 5:3H. R. Papa now offers
    an alternative explanation for the repetition.] R. Papa said, "[The rule is
    apparently repeated because in fact] they [sages in A-B and Rabbi in H]
    disagree about unblemished Holy Things dedicated to the altar which became
    blemished and [which were then] wrongly slaughtered;

H. "for has it not been taught [on Tannaitic authority]: '[As regards]
    unblemished holy things [designated for] the altar which became blemished and

were [then] wrongly slaughtered—Rabbi says they bury it [because it cannot
be redeemed. Burying it is thus the only way to protect it from ever being
used, Cf. Hullin 30a. Since it cannot be deconsecrated, it follows that it
is subject to sacrilege following sacrilege. This is Rabbi's view in H.]
Sages say they may redeem it.' [Since the animal can be redeemed, it follows
that it is not subject to sacrilege following sacrilege. This is sages view
in A-B.]"

At issue in Mishnah is the status of a consecrated object that has
inadvertently been used for a secular purpose. According to sages in M. 5:3A-B,
the act of misusing such a consecrated item renders the item secular (except in
the case of beasts and the holy utensils). It follows that such an item is no
longer subject to sacrilege. Rabbi in M. 5:3H states matters differently,
claiming that only if the item may be deconsecrated is it made secular. If it
cannot be deconsecrated, it retains its consecrated status, and so its
suceptibility to sacrilege. Gemara wants to know whether these two statements of
the law are in fact substantively different. After identifying the authority
behind Mishnah's anonymous rule in 5:3A-B (unit I), unit II explores the possible
differences entailed in these two formulations.

5:4-5

A. [If] one took a stone or a beam from what is consecrated, lo, this one has
   not committed an act of sacrilege.

B. [20A] [If] he gave it to his fellow, he has committed an act of sacrilege,

C. but his fellow has not committed an act of sacrilege.

D. [If] he built it into the structure of his house, lo, this one has not
   commited an act of sacrilege—

E. until he actually will live under it [and enjoy its use] to the extent of a
   perutah's worth.

F. [If] he took a perutah of consecrated money, lo, this one has not committed
   an act of sacrilege.

G. [If] he gave it to his fellow, he has committed an act of sacrilege.

H. But his fellow has not committed an act of sacrilege.

I. [If] he gave it to a bath-keeper, even though he did not take a bath, he has

committed an act of sacrilege.

J. For he [the bath-keeper] says to him, "Lo, the bath is open to you. Go in

and take a bath."

M. 5:4

A. What he has eaten and what his fellow has eaten,

B. what he has used and what his fellow has used,

C. what he has eaten and what his fellow has used,

D. what he has used and what his fellow has eaten

E. join together with one another--

F. and even over an extended period of time.

M. 5:5

I.

A. Why distinguish [in Mishnah 5:5] between what one does and what one's fellow
does?

B. Said Samuel, "[We distinguish because] we are dealing here with the Temple-
treasurer with whom the goods are deposited." [If he himself uses Holy Things
for his own benefit, no sacrilege occurs because the goods are still being
used in the holy domain. If he shares the goods with another, however, then
the goods are used outside the holy domain, and the laws of sacrilege are
violated.]

II.

A. [Turning to M. 5:4 D: If] he built it into the structure of his house, lo
this one is not liable [for transgressing the laws of sacrilege] until he
actually will live under it:

B. Why [is he not liable] until he actually will live under it? [Surely when he
builds it into his houses] he changes [its character and] thereby commits
sacrilege.

C. Said Rab, "[An act of sacrilege is committed only when he derives benefit from it.] If he simply lays it over a roof-opening [he has not yet derived any benefit and so has committed no sacrilege]."

D. But simply by building it into his house does he not commit sacrilege?

E. I say the following supports Rab [that simply using the beam to cover a hole does not constitute sacrilege]: For Rab said, "Only when one bows to a house, does that structure become prohibited [as an idol." This change in status occurs not when the structure is built, but only when someone actually makes use of it.]

F. Said R. Aha son of R. Iqa, "[Rab's argument in E is irrelevant.] Torah forbids only publically deriving benefit [from an idolatrous object. Thus openly bowing to the house renders it prohibited. But as regards sacrilege, even deriving private benefit constitutes sacrilege, so that even just using the beam to cover a hole is prohibited.]

G. I say the following also supports [Rab]: "One dwelling in a consecrated house commits sacrilege simply because he derives benefit thereby. [That is, the mere fact that one lives in a house that contains a consecrated beam constitutes sacrilege ipso facto.]"

H. Said Resh Laqish, [rejecting this warrant for Rab's view], "This refers to a case in which the material was consecrated and then he built the structure. [By living there, he is deriving benefit from the consecrated materials.] But what if he built the structure and then consecrated the material? In this case, he commits no act of sacrilege [because he does not derive any added benefit from the materials once they are consecrated]."

I. [Resh Laqish's rejoinder to Rab is now given support.] Why was it necessary to teach [the following]: "One living in a cave chamber [consecrated to the Temple] does not thereby commit an act of sacrilege"? Why not teach, "One living in a house of stone which was built and then consecrated, does not thereby commit an act of sacrilege"? [That is, what is the point of constructing a teaching about a cave, when the issue at hand has to do with the use of consecrated building materials.]

M.   They said, "[The reason is to prove Resh Laqish's point. The case of the
     cave] is clearcut [in that the cave was obviously there before it was
     consecrated. This unequivocally shows that no sacrilege is committed if one
     lives in a dwelling that was consecrated after its construction. On the
     other hand, the case of the stone house] is not clearcut [since it is
     possible to argue that the house was originally built out of consecrated
     stones. In order to make the case crystal clear, then, we frame the ruling
     as regards a cave, so that there can be no doubt that if the dwelling first
     exists and then is subsequently consecrated, dwelling in it thereafter does
     not constitute sacrilege.]"

     Talmud investigates the two salient points in Mishnah's rulings. Unit I
     explains why M. 5:5 distinguishes between what the guardian of the consecrated
     item does with that item and what someone else does with it. There is a
     difference, Gemara explains because the guardian is acting on behalf of the
     Temple while the commoner derives personal benefit from its use. With this in
     mind, Unit II turns to M. 5:4, investigating in detail the point at which one can
     be said to derive personal benefit from a consecrated object, in this case, as
     construction material in a house.

A. The agent who carried out his errand [and thereby inadvertently committed an act of sacrilege—]

B. the householder [who appointed the agent is responsible and] has committed the act of sacrilege.

C. [If the agent] did not carry out his errand [in committing an act of sacrilege].

D. The agent [is responsible and inadvertently] has committed the act of sacrilege.

E. How so?

F. [If] he said to him, "Give out meat to the guests," but he gave them liver,

G. "Liver," and he gave them meat—

H. The agent has committed the act of sacrilege.

I. [If] he said to him, "Give them one piece each," and he [the agent] said, "Take two each," but they took three each,

J. all of them are guilty of committing an act of sacrilege.

I.

A. [20B] Who is the Tanna who taught that any matter about which the agent must consult his employer is deemed to be a distinct act? [That is, if an act is not clearly what the master hand in mind, such that clarification is necessary, then this act is deemed to be done on the agent's personal initiative. If it involves sacrilege, the master is not responsible.]

B. Said R. Hisda, "This cannot be R. Aqiba, for we learn [in M. Ned. 7:1]: 'If one swears not to eat vegetables, he may eat squash [since their status as a vegtable is in doubt]. But Aqiba forbids [eating squash because the squash may be considered a vegetable. His view, then, is that if the act is not clearly different from what the oath-taker intended, then it is deemed covered by the oath. Likewise if an act is not clearly different from a master's commission, then it must be deemed part of that commission.]

C. Abayye said, "But can you [not say that Aqiba forbids the squash only because in a case of doubt] the agent should ask the master [and not because in a case of doubt, the squash is covered by the oath]?"

D. When our rabbis reported [this retort] to Raba, he said, "Nahmani [i.e., Abayye] spoke well."

E. Who is the Tanna who opposes R. Aqiba [by claiming that in a case of doubt, an act is not deemed to be covered by the oath]?

F. It is R. Simeon b. Gamaliel. For it is taught, "If one foreswears meat, this one is prohibited [from eating] any kinds of meat as well as [from eating] the head, the legs, the gullet, the liver, and the heart; and the flesh of fowl—although he may eat fish and locust. But R. Simeon b. Gamaliel allows the head, the legs, the gullet, the liver of fowl and fish and locust, [because there is doubt as to whether these are meat, and so they are not covered by the oath].

G. Also did Rabban Simeon b. Gamaliel say, "Entrails are not meat, and those who eat them are not [proper] people."

H. Why does the first authority [in F prohibit] fowl [to one who has foresworn "meat"]?

I. [He prohibits fowl] because people generally [consider it to be meat] saying, [for example,] "I could find no red meat, so I brought fowl."

J. If this is so, then the same should be [true for fish], for people say, "I could find no red meat, so I brought fish." [Yet according to this authority, one can foreswear "meat" and still eat fish.]

K. Said R. Papa, "[The reason we allow one who foreswears meat to eat fish is that usually such vows] are made when one is having blood let, and one would not eat fish [then anyway." The oath is taken to apply only to what one would normally eat at that time, namely, red meat and fowl.]

L. [But then we should allow him to eat fowl as well after such an oath,] for fowl [like fish] is not eaten [on the day one has blood let]!

M. This is as Samuel [a physician] said [indicating that people do not eat fowl after a bloodletting], "If one who has had blood let eats fowl, his heart will flutter like a bird."

N. And further it has been taught [on Tannaitic authority]: "One does not let
   blood [after eating] fish or fowl or salted meat." [This shows that fowl and
   fish are alike as regards letting blood, and not to be distinguished from red
   meat.]

O. Said R. Papa, "[In fact, my statement in K] applies only when [one has blood
   let and afterwards] his eyes hurt. In this case one does not eat fish [which
   is bad for the eyes. But since people otherwise generally eat fish after a
   bloodletting, fish may be regarded as a meat." Thus to be consistent, the
   first authority in F should prohibit both fish and fowl after an oath not to
   eat meat.]

II.

A. [Turning to M. 6:1 I-J]: If he said to him, "Give them one piece each," and
   he [the agent] said, "Take two each," but they took three each, all of them
   are guilty of committing an act of sacrilege:

B. We infer from this that even though the agent adds to his commission [by
   offering each guest two pieces], he is still in the status of agent [such
   that the master bears responsibility for the resulting sacrilege].

C. Said R. Sheshet, "[Our Mishnah-passage assumes] that the agent said, 'Take
   one piece of meat on my master's authority and one on my authority.'

D. [21A] "Now you might think that in such a case the agent cancels [his status
   as] an agent such that the master no longer bears responsibility for the act
   of sacrilege [that follows].

E. "[Our Mishnah-passage thus] comes to teach that this is in fact not the case
   [and the master continues to bear responsibility]."

   If an agent commits an act of sacrilege in the course of carrying out his
commission, he is not liable, responsibility falling on the one who sent him. If
it is clear that the agent was acting on his own, however, he does bear
responsibility. This is the simple meaning of M. 6:1. Unit I asks who is
responsible if the agent is engaged in an act similar to, but not exactly
identical with, his commission. This leads directly to Unit II's examination of
M. 6:1I-J, which presents a case in which the agent and the master both end up
bearing responsibility.

6:1K–6:2

K. [If] he said to him: "Bring [such and such a thing] from the window or from
the chest," and he brought it to him [from somewhere else],

L. even though the householder said, "I meant *only* from here, and he brought it
from there,"

M. the householder has committed the act of sacrilege.

N. But if he said to him, "Bring it to me from the window," but he brought it
from the chest,

O. or "From the chest," and he brought it from the window––

P. the agent has committed the act of sacrilege.

6:1K–P

A. [If] he sent by means of [an agent who was] a deaf-mute, an imbecile, or a
minor [to purchase goods with money which unbeknownst to the sender, was
consecrated],

B. if they carried out their errand,

C. the householder has committed an act of sacrilege,

D. [If] they did not carry out their errand,

E. the storekeeper has committed the act of sacrilege.

F. [If] he sent [consecrated coins] by means of a person of sound senses,

G. and realized before he reached the storekeeper [that the coins are
consecrated and therefore regretted having sent those coins],

H. the storekeeper will have committed the act of sacrilege when he pays out
[the coins].

I. What should he [F–G] do?

J. He should take a perutah or a utensil and state, "A perutah which is
consecrated, wherever it may be, is made unconsecrated by this."

K. For that which is consecrated is redeemed by money or by something which is
worth money.

M. 6:2

I.

A. What does [M. 6:1K-L] teach us?

B. [It teaches] that unexpressed thoughts have no status.

II.

A. [Turning to M. 6:2A-C:] If he sent by means of [an agent who was] a deaf-mute, an imbecile, or a minor and if they carried out their errand. . . [the householder has committed an act of sacrilege:

B. [Why talk about deaf-mutes, etc., since] lo, they cannot be agents [in the first place]!

C. Said R. Eleazar, "[They function as agents in the same way as does] the olive vat. For we have taught: When [do we assume the owner has purposely dampened] olives so that they become susceptible to food-uncleanness? When they exude juice in a vat, [since the vat preserves the juice] but not when they exude juice in a basket, [since the basket allows the juice to run off (Toh. 9:1)." Thus the action of the vat renders the olives susceptible, meaning that the vat has in effect acted as an agent of the owner.]

D. R. Yohanan said, "This is the same principle [as the following] we have learned: If one placed [food and drink] on an ape or on an elephant, and this [animal] takes it [to a designated place] where another is designated to receive them, lo [it is as if the person himself carried the food and drink to that spot and they can be used there to create a] Sabbath-limit [for the person who sent them]. From this we conclude that just as the [animal] acts as an agent so too can agency be carried out [by a deaf-mute, imbecile, or minor]."

III.

A. [Turning to M. 6:2F-H:] If he sent [consecrated coins to a shopkeeper by means of an agent] of sound sense, [and realized before the agent arrived that the coins were consecrated, the shopkeeper commits an act of sacrilege when he pays out the coins]:

B. [We conclude that this is so] even if the agent did not realize [that the coins were consecrated and so handed them over as secular coins. Thus even

if the shopkeeper changed his mind after the agent left, the agent is still
fulfilling his commission, and the shopkeeper is responsibile for the
sacrilege that follows.]

C. The following contradicts [this conclusion]: "If the householder realized
[that the coins are consecrated], but the agent did not, then the agent
commits the act of sacrilege [for he uses the coins with the wrong intention.
This is exactly the contrary of B.] If both [the householder and the agent]
realize [that the coins are consecrated] then the shopkeeper commits the act
of sacrilege."

D. Said R. Sheshet, "[There is no necessary contradiction. We can simply say
that] M. 6:2H [assumes] that both [the householder and the agent] realized
[that the coins are consecrated, so that the shopkeeper commits the act of
sacrilege. In this way B and C are consistent.]"

The operative principle here has already been articulated in M. 6:1A—J.   It
is that an agent that commits a sacrilege in the course of carrying out his
commission is not liable since he is acting only on behalf of his employer. In
this case, the employer is liable. If the agent does something on his own,
however, and that act constitutes sacrilege, then the agent is liable. M.6:1K—L
carry this theme forward by noting that any act the agent carries out that stands
within the general meaning of the employer's charge is the responsibility of the
employer, even if the employer had mental reservations. It is the actual stated
words that govern the case. This is the point of Unit I. Unit II directs our
attention to the next item on Mishnah's agendum, explaining why M. 6:2A—C
discusses the effect of deaf—mutes, imbeciles and minors, since these can not in
any event act as legal agents. Unit III, finally, turns to Mishnah's third
thematic block, M.6:2F—K. Here Mishnah presents a case in which the employer
gave his agent a charge and then, after the agent has left, changed his mind.
Talmud explains why in this case the householder remains liable.

6:3-4

A. [If] he gave him a perutah [and] said to him,

B. "With half of it bring me lamps, and with half of it wicks,"

C. and [if] he went and brought back lamps for the whole of it or wicks for the whole of it--

D. or if he said to him, "Bring me lamps for the whole of it," or, "Wicks for the whole of it,"

E. and he went and brought him lamps for half of it and wicks for half of it,

F. both of them have not committed an act of sacrilege.

G. But if he said to him, "Bring me lamps for half of it from such-and-such a place, and wicks for half of it from such-and-such a place,"

H. and he went and brought for him lamps from the place from which he was supposed to get the wicks, and wicks from the place from which he was supposed to get the lamps,

I. the agent has committed the act of sacrilege.

M.6:3

A. If he gave him two perutot [and] said to him, "Bring me an etrog,"

B. and he went and brought him an etrog for a perutah and a pomegranate for a perutah.

C. both of them have committed the act of sacrilege.

D. R. Judah says, "The householder has not committed an act of sacrilege.

E. "For he says to him, 'I want a big etrog, and you brought a small and poor one'"

F. [If] he gave him a golden dinar [six selas] [and] said to him, "Bring me a shirt,"

G. [21B]and he went and brought him a shirt for three selas and a cloak for three,

H. both of them have committed an act of sacrilege.

I. R. Judah says, "The householder has not committed an act of sacrilege.

J. "For he says to him, 'I want a large shirt, and you brought me a small and poor one.'"

M. 6:4

I.

A. Do you infer from [M. 6:4F-H] that if one says to his agent, "Go buy me a <u>kor</u> of land," but [the agent] goes and buys only a <u>letek</u> [that is, half a <u>kor</u>], that the purchaser has acquired the land [even though his instructions were not followed]?

B. [No. The sages in our Mishnah-passage] say that [normally if a commission is not carried out, the master is not responsible for any act of sacrilege that results. The case before us, however, is like the master who tells his agent to buy a shirt for six <u>selas</u>, and the servant buys one for three <u>selas</u>. The master acquires the shirt] because it is as if the servant bought for the three <u>selas</u> a shirt worth six <u>selas</u> [and so, in effect, carries out the master's instructions].

C. [This is not so] for let me cite the last clause [M. 6:4I-J], which says, <u>R. Judah says, "The householder has not committed an act of sacrilege because he can [still] say to him, 'I wanted a large shirt, but you brought me a small and poor one.'"</u> [Accordingly, the masters in A and B would not acquire the land or the shirt.]

D. [That is, the householder] is saying to him [the agent: "Although you bought a shirt worth six <u>selas</u> for only three <u>selas</u>,] had you spent the whole dinar [= six <u>selas</u>, as I told you], you could have bought [an even nicer shirt, one worth] two dinars. [Since you did not <u>spend</u> what I told you, you bought a poorer shirt than necessary, and so have not followed my instructions.]"

E. [We now show that the rules of A and B are correct; the master does acquire the purchases. These rules are] consistent with [what Judah] teaches in the last clause [of Tosefta 2:10]: "R. Judah agrees that [if the master gives the agent a dinar with which to buy] pulse [and the agent spends the full amount], both commit an act of sacrilege, whether [the agent] buys [a quantity] of pulse worth a <u>dinar</u> or [a quantity] worth a <u>perutah</u>."

F. Why [does the quantity he buys differ so widely]? In a place where they sell pulse by estimate [i.e., wholesale] surely if he gives them a <u>sela</u>, they will sell it to him more cheaply [than if he buys only a small quantity at a time].

G. Said R. Papa, "[The quantity is irrelevant to Judah, because he assumes] the
    sale takes place where they sell [pulse] by the measure, each measure for one
    perutah, such that the price is fixed." [Thus what a dinar will buy varies,
    depending on the market. In either case, the agent has followed his
    commission by spending the amount of money he was given, irregardless of how
    much he was given in return.]

    Mishnah continues its investigation of agency. A householder gives an agent
a fixed amount of money to buy some item. The agent only uses part of the money
for the requested item. Mishnah declares that this a valid act of agency such
that the householder who sent the agent acquires the items in question. Judah
holds, on the other hand, that no act of agency occurred since the agent did not
do as he was bid--spend the full amount of money--but acted on his own.   Talmud
establishes the cogency of the first position, that the agent's deeds constitute
a valid fulfillment of his commission. In terms of the theme of our tractate,
this means that should the agent in such a case be committing a sacrilege, the
master would bear responsibility.

                                    6:5-6

A. He who deposits coins with a money-changer--

B. if they were bound up, he [the money-changer] should not make use of them.

C. Therefore if he paid [them] out, he has committed an act of sacrilege.

D. If they are loose, he may make use of them.

E. Therefore if he paid them out, he has not committed an act of sacrilege.

F. [If the owner of the coins] deposited [them] with a householder,

G. one way or the other, he [the householder] should not make use of them.

H. Therefore if he paid them out, he has committed an act of sacrilege.

I. "A storekeeper is deemed equivalent to a householder," the words of R. Meir.

J. R. Judah says, "He is equivalent to a money-changer."

                                    M. 6:5

A. A perutah which has been consecrated, which fell into a purse [containing
    other money],

B. or if one said, "A perutah in this purse is consecrated"--

C. "as soon as one paid out the first [coin in the purse],

D. "he has committed an act of sacrilege," the words of R. Aqiba

E. And sages say, "[He has not committed an act of sacrilege] until he has paid
    out all the money in the purse."

F. And R. Aqiba concedes in the case of one who says, "A perutah in this purse
    is consecrated," that he goes along and pays out the money [without having
    committed an act of sacrilege] until he will have paid out all the money
    which is in the purse.

M. 6:6

I.

A. When R. Dimi arrived [from Palestine], he reported that Resh Laqish had asked
    of R. Yohanan: "Why is there a difference between [Aqiba's view] in the
    first clause [M. 6:6 C-E, where he deems the householder to commit an act of
    sacrilege as soon as he pays out the first coin] and [his view] in the second
    clause [M. 6:6F, where he deems the householder to commit an act of
    sacrilege only when he pays out all the coins]?"

B. [Yohanan] said to him, "In the second clause, [the owner] says that not [all
    the money in] the purse is to be exempted from being dedicated [to the
    Temple." Thus as long as at least one coin remains in the purse to be
    consecrated, no act of sacrilege occurs. In contrsat, we know in A-E that
    one of the coins is consecrated, so that as soon as one is spent, we must
    suspect that an act of sacrilege has occurred.]

C. When Rabin arrived [from Palestine], he said, "[Resh Laqish also] pointed
    out a contradiction between the rule concerning oxen and [Aqiba's] rule
    concerning coins. For we teach, 'One who says, 'One of my oxen is dedicated
    [to the Temple]' but he has at least two oxen, then the bigger is
    [automatically deemed] dedicated [to the Temple.' As regards coins, however,
    Aqiba in F does not declare that the finest perutah is deemed to be the one
    that is consecrated.]"

D. He [Yohanan] said to him, "[There is no contradiction,] for the latter
    clause, [M. 6:6F] concerns one who said, 'The money in this purse shall not
    be totally exempt from being dedicated [to the Temple.' That is, the owner of
    the purse did not yet consecrate a specific coin. We thus assume he means to
    consecrate only the last coin in the purse.]

E. [22A] Said R. Papa, "[Resh Laqish further] pointed out a contradiction
    between the rule for logs [of wine] and [Aqiba's] rule for coins in a
    purse;

F. "for we teach, 'One who buys [100 logs of] wine from the Cutheans says, 'Two
    logs which I shall ultimately set aside are [hereby designated as] heave-
    offering, ten [logs are hereby designated as] first tithe, nine [logs as]
    second tithe.' He may then redeem the latter [i.e., the nine logs designated
    as second tithe] and drink them immediately,' the words of R. Meir. [But] R.
    Judah and R. Yose and R. Simeon forbid [drinking any of the wine until all
    consecrated portion of the wine has been physically removed." This seems to
    contradict M. 6:6F, for Aqiba allows one who has declared a coin to be
    consecrated to use some of the coins before he physically removes the coin he
    dedicated to the Temple.]

G. He [Yohanan] said to him, "[There is no contradiction here either, for the
    later clause [M. 6:6F] concerns one who said, 'The money in this purse shall
    not be totally exempt from being dedicated [to the Temple.' That is, the
    owner did not consecrated any particular coin yet, and so there is nothing to
    be removed.]"

At issue in talmud is Aqiba's rule in M. 6:6F. Resh Laqish challenges
Aqiba's rule on three grounds (given at A, C and E-F). Each objection is
successfully countered (B,D and G), showing Aqiba's rule to be cogent.

Mishnah Tamid consists of a narrative description of the daily routine of the Jerusalem Temple as Mishnah's authors imagine it. It is of interest to the authorities of the Gemara only insofar as it intersects with, and stands in contradiction to, the description of the Temple compound known from another Mishnaic tractate, Middot. Talmud's authorities are interested in reconciling the material found in these two Mishnaic tractates whenever they appear to be in conflict. The following outline indicates the major topics covered in Mishnah Tamid:

I. Preparing the altar in the morning (1:1-2:5)

    A. The Priests arise in the morning (1:1-4)

        1:1 In three places do the priests keep watch

        1:2 He who wants to clean the ashes gets up early

        1:3 Opening the door and initial inspection

        1:4 The one who wins the right to clear the ashes

    B. Clearing the altar (2:1-5)

        2:1 Priests help clear the altar

        2:2 They heap up the ashes

        2:3 They heap up twigs for the altar-fire

        2:4-5 Priests arrange the altar-fire

II. Selecting the lamb for the daily burnt-offering (3:1-5)

        3:1 The superintendent casts lots to assign jobs

        3:2 Superintendent determines that the time of the rite has come

        3:3 The lamb is selected

3:4 The utensils for slaughter are taken out

3:5 The lamb is brought to the shambles

III. Clearing the altar (3:6-9)

3:6-8 The priestly procession

3:9 The ashes are removed and the candlestick cleaned

IV. Slaughtering the lamb (4:1-3)

V.   The Priests bless the congregation. The limbs are brought to the altar (5:1-5:4)

A. Blessing (5:1)

B. Carrying the limbs (5:2-4)

5:2 Lots are cast to choose a priest

5:3 Other priests are dismissed

5:4 Incense is offered

VI. Clearing the ashes (5:5-6:3)

5:5-6 The ashes are removed and disposed of

6:1 The incense is placed

6:2 The cinders are heaped up

6:3 The incense is prepared

VII. Conclusion of the rite (7:1-4)

7:1 The High Priest prostrates himself

7:2 The Priests line up on the steps of the porch

7:3 The rite is carried out

7:4 What psalms the Levites said

As the outline indicates, only the first four chapters cover material that is also found in tractate Middot, namely the layout of the Temple compound and of the altar area. Consequently, the commentary of Gemara, which, as we said is interested in reconciling M. Tamid with M. Middot, can extend only to these four chapters. Because Chapter Three is concerned with substantially the same area as is Chapter Two, we find Amoraic material only for Chapters One, Two and Four. In adition to reconciling Mishnah Tamid and Mishnah Middot, Gemara also supplies Scriptural warrant for some of Mishnah's descriptions. Beyond these simple tasks, no fresh intellectual initiatives are undertaken.

This translation follows the same format as that of Me'ilah (see the Introduction there). Along with the commentary of RASHI, I regularly consulted the the translation of Maurice Simon in Tamid. Translated into English with Notes, Glossary and Indices. (London: Soncino, 1948). The translation of Mishnah and the outline above are taken, with minor adjustments, from J. Neusner, A History of the Mishnaic Law of Holy Things. Part Five (Leiden: Brill, 1980).

CHAPTER NINE

BAVLI TAMID CHAPTER ONE

1:1-2

A. [25B] In three places do the priests keep watch in the sanctuary: (1) in the room of Abtinas, (2) in the room of the flame, and (3) in the room of the hearth.

B. The room of Abtinas and the room of the flame were upper rooms

C. and youngsters keep watch there.

D. The room of the hearth is vaulted.

E. And it was a large room surrounded by a raised pavement of stone.

F. And the mature members of the [priestly] household [of the day] sleep there [on the raised pavement],

G. with the keys to the courtyard in their charge,

H. and [there sleep] the fledgling priests, each with his mattress on the ground.

I. They [the priests] did not sleep in consecrated garments.

J. But they spread them out, doubled them over, and lay them down under their heads, and cover themselves with their own clothes.

K. [If] one of them should have a nocturnal emission of semen, he goes out, [26A] proceeding along the passage that leads below the building—

L. and lamps flicker on this side and on that—

M. until he reaches the immersion-room,

N. and there was a fire there,

O. and a privy in good taste.

P. And this was its good taste: [if] he found it locked, he knows that someone is there: [if he found it] open, he knows that no one is there,

Q. He went down and immersed, came up and dried off, and warmed himself by the fire.

R. He came and sat down with his brothers, the priests [in the house of the hearth],

S. until the gates were opened.

T. He goes out, proceeding on his way [home].

                        M. 1:1

A. He who wants to take up [the ashes] from the altar gets up early,

B. and immerses before the superintendent comes by.

C. And at what times does the superintendent come by?

D. Not all the times are the same.

E. Sometimes he comes at cockcrow, or near then, earlier or later.

F. The superintendent came and knocked on their door.

G. And they opened it for him.

H. He said to them, "Let him who has immersed come and cast lots."

I. They cast lots.

J. Whoever won, won.

                        M. 1:2

I.

A. From where [in Scripture do we know that there are three places in which the
    watch is kept, M. 1:1A]?

B. Said Abayye, "Scripture (Nu 3:38) says, 'Those camping near the tabernacle to
    the east, that is, eastward of the tent of meeting--Moses, Aaron and his
    sons--are to keep watch of the Sanctuary, a watch on behalf of the Children
    of Israel.'" [Moses, Aaron, and Aaron's son comprise three watches.]

C. They say, "The watch [of Moses] does not count as a normal watch ('yn symwr
    b'lm') for we find that a watch always requires priests [B. adds: and
    Levites] [and Moses was not a priest. So Numbers 3:38 provides warrant for
    only two watches.]"

D. [To the contrary,] our Mishnah [Middot 1:1] teaches: In three places do the
    priests keep watch in the sanctuary, and the Levites in twenty-one
    [indicating that there can be watches made up of only Levites, such as
    Moses]!

E. Perhaps [Mishnah] is using "priest" and "Levite" interchangeably here [so
    that in fact only Priests can make up a watch]?

F. They say, "[We can still read Scripture to require three priestly watches, for Scripture says,] 'Those camping near the Tabernacle to the east, that is, eastward of the tent of meeting of Moses. . . .' It then goes on to say, 'Aaron and his sons are to keep watch of the Sanctuary.' [We infer from this] that Aaron serves in one place and his sons [plural] in [at least] two others [thus making up three watches of priests in all]."

G. How do we know this [interprtation is correct]?

H. [We know] because "camping" is written [as regards Moses] and "keeping watch" is written [as regards Aaron and his sons. It follows that] those camping [Moses] are regarded separately and those watching [Aaron and his sons] are regarded separately.

I. [But what if I were to say that they camped and kept watch] all together in one place?

J. Do not entertain this thought! Just as Moses has his own camping place, so too do Aaron and his sons have their own camping place.

K. R. Ashi said, "[You can infer that there are three watches also from] the last clause of our Scripture passage [i.e., Nu. 3:38, which says], 'keep' (swmrym), 'watch' (msmrt) and 'for a watch' (lmsmrt). [These three words indicate that three different watches are meant.]

II.

A. [26B][Turning to M. 1:1B:] The room of Abtinas and the room of the flame [were upper rooms]:

B. It was asked of them, "Were these really upper rooms [i.e., attics] or were they only raised [above the ground] like upper rooms?"

C. Come and hear [the answer], for we have learned: And that on the north side is the gate of the flame. And it was like a portico with an upper chamber built on it through which the priests keep watch from above, and the Levites from below. And it has a door leading out to the rampart [M. Mid. 1:5]. [This shows it was a real attic.]

D. From where [in Scripture] is it inferred [that the priests keep watch in an upper chamber and the Levites in a lower one]?

E. Our rabbis teach, "[Nu. 18:2 says,] 'So that they [the Levites] may accompany you [the priests] and serve you.' [By stating matters in the way, Scripture

means to show that the Levites serve] your particular labor [that is, the
priests' labor is unique and so they alone use the special upper chamber]."

F. You might retort, "Does Scripture indeed mean your [the priests' particular]
service, or does it mean their [priests' and Levites'] common service [i.e.,
that both keep watch together in the upper chamber]?"

G. [It means the priests work alone,] for when [Nu. 18:4 says], "They shall
accompany you and keep charge over [the Tent of Meeting]," lo it refers to
their [common] service. How then am I to interpret the words "so that they
may accompany you and serve you?" [I interprete this to mean that] Scripture
is referring specifically to your [the priests'] particular service.

H. And how [is such a distinction maintained]? By the priests keeping watch
from an upper chamber and the Levites from a lower one.

III.

A. [Turning to M. 1:1D:] The room of the hearth is vaulted. And it was a large
room. . . :

B. There was only one watch kept in the room of the hearth.

C. They challenged him [on the basis of the following]: There were two gates in
the room of the hearth, one opening to the rampart and one opening to the
Temple courtyard. Said R. Judah, 'In the one through which they enter onto
the courtyard there was a small doorway through which they would enter to
inspect the courtyard' [M. Mid. 1:7]. [The inference is that since there
were two gates to be watched, there must also have been at least two
guards.]

D. Said Abayye, "Since the two gates were close together, one watch was
sufficient, the guard being able to glance the from one to the other."

IV.

A. [Turning to M. 1:1E: And it was a large room] surrounded by a raised
pavement of stone [M. Mid. 1:8A]:

B. What is [meant by] "a raised pavement?"

C. These were shaped stones for the berths, upon which they would climb to reach
the berths.

D. But did they indeed shape stones [for use in the Temple]? Is it not written
   (1 King 6:7), "When the house was built, only finished stones cut at the
   quarry were used, [meaning that no stones were shaped within the Temple
   compound]"?

E. Said Abayye, "They prepared ahead of time big slabs and little slabs to bring
   [to the construction site to make the pavement]. This is as is written (1
   King 7:10), 'stones of eight and of ten cubits.'"

V.

A. [Turning to M. 1:1F:] And the mature members of the [priestly] household
   [of the day] sleep there [on the pavement] [Cf M. Mid. 1:8B]:

B. And why [did they sleep on the pavement]? Let them bring in beds!

C. Said Abayye, "[They slept on the pavement because] it was not deemed proper
   to bring beds into the sanctuary."

VI.

A. [Turning to M. 1:1H:] And [there sleep] the fledgling priests, each with his
   mattress [pr.ed. has "garment"] on the ground [M. Mid. 1:8C]:

B. Why were they called "youngsters" there [M. 1:1C] but [27A] "fledgling
   priests" here?

C. They say, "This is a correct [usage]. There, when they were not yet ready to
   perform the service they are called 'youngsters.' Here, when they have
   become ready to perform the service, they are called 'fledgling priests.'"

VII.

A. We taught there [M. Mid. 1:1]: In three places do the priests keep watch in
   the sanctuary: (1) in the room of Abtinas, (2) in the room of the flame, (3)
   in the room of the hearth. And the Levites [keep watch] in twenty-one
   places: five at the five gates of the Temple mount; four at the four corners
   on the inside [of the Temple-wall]; five at the five gates of the courtyard;
   four at the four corners on the outside [wall of the courtyard]; and one at
   the office of the offering, and one at the office of the veil; and one behind
   the Mercy Seat [outside of the western wall of the Holy of Holies]:

B. From where [in Scripture] is all this derived?

C. Said R. Judah of Sura—but some say it is taught in another Tannaitic source—
   —,"It is written (1 Chron. 26:17f), 'On the east were six Levites, on the

north there were four per day, on the south were four per day, for the storehouses there were two each and for the <u>Parbar</u> there were four on the west at the road and two at the <u>Parbar</u> [itself].' [Adding these numbers together gives us the number of Levitical watches]."

D. They said, "But this [adds up to] twenty-four [while Mishnah staes that there were only twenty-one]!"

E. Said Abayye, "This is what is meant: 'for the storehouses [a <u>total</u> of two]' [rather than 'two each'. This gives us two less]."

F. But if so we still have twenty-two [instead of the twenty-one specified by Mishnah].

G. [We can reduce this number further by examining] how matters worked at the <u>Parbar</u>.

H. For there was only one [Levite actually] on duty there, [rather than the two claimed at C.] The other [Levite] was there simply to keep him company. He would go and sit with [the Levite on duty] because the Levite on duty was outside [alone. Thus we have only twenty-one Levites actually on watch.]

I. [And this is born out by the meaning of "<u>parbar</u>"], for what does "<u>parbar</u>" mean?

J. Said Rabbah b. R. Shila, "It is as if one says, 'Outside [<u>kalpe bar</u>]'"!

K. If you insist [I can reconcile matters another way]. Scripture does enumerate twenty-four positions [as in C-D]: three of these for the priests and twenty-one for the Levites. [These are the twenty-one ennumerated in Mishnah.]

L. [This reconciliation must be rejected, because Scripture] clearly is referring to Levites [alone and not to priests].

M. [We can counter this objection] along the lines of R. Joshua b. Levi, for R. Joshua ben Levi said, "In twenty-four places [in Scripture] the priests are called 'Levites,' [Thus the word 'Levites' can include priests.]"

N. This is one of the clearest examples: "The Levitical priests, sons of Sadoq (Ezekiel 44:15)."

VIII.

A. [Turning to M. Middot 1:1C-F:] <u>Five of the five gates of the Temple mount; four at the four corners on the inside; five at the five gates of the</u>

courtyard; and four at the four corners on the outside....:

B. What is the difference between the Temple-mount, where we serve on the
    inside, and the courtyard, where we serve on the outside?

C. They answer, "On the Temple mount, if [the guard] feels tired and wants to
    sit down, he may sit down. Thus we say, 'He is inside.' In the courtyard,
    if he feels tired and wants to sit down, he may not do so [for he is outside,
    open to public view];

D. "for the master said, 'There is no sitting allowed in the courtyard except
    for kings of the House of David only, therefore we say, '[This priest] is
    outside.'''"

E. Said the master, "[M. Mid.1:1E says,] five at the five gates of the
    courtyard. Were there really only five gates to the courtyard?

F. "This is contradicted by [M. Mid. 1:4 A-B which says], Seven gates were in
    the courtyard: three on the north, three on the south, and one on the east."

G. Said Abayye, "Two [of the seven gates] did not need to be guarded." [Thus
    when enumerating the watches, M. Mid. 1:1 needs to list only five gates.]

H. Raba said, "[The precise number of gates is a matter of dispute] among the
    Tannaitic authorities. For it is taught [in Shek. 5:2], They appoint no
    fewer than thirteen [M. Sheq. has 'three'] revenuers and seven supervisors.
    [On the basis of this passage,] R. Nathan says, 'They appoint no fewer than
    thirteen revenuers, corresponding to the thirteen gates [of the Temple].
    Take away the five on the Temple mount, and you have eight gates left for the
    courtyard.'

I. "We see therefore that there is a Tannaitic authority who says that there are
    eight [gateways leading into the courtyard--namely, R. Nathan in H], a
    Tannaitic authority who says there are seven [E-F], and a Tannaitic authority
    who says there are five [the authority behind M. 1:1C]."

IX.

A. [Reverting to M. Tamid 1:1/I:] They did not sleep in consecrated garments:

B. [Although] sleeping was not done [in them, Mishnah implies], they did walk
    around in them. From this you could conclude that priestly garments were
    available [to the priests for personal] benefit.

C. They said, "The law is [in fact] that even walking around was not to be done
   [in these garments]. Mishnah said, they do not sleep in consecrated garments
   only because it wanted to say afterwards but they spread them out, doubled
   them over and lay them down under their heads. [Since Mishnah allows priests
   to lie down on their garments in the second clause, it] says explicitly in
   the first clause, they did not sleep. . ." [The phrase "they do not sleep
   in them" is meant to qualify the following phrase and does not mean to imply
   that the priests may use the garments for personal benefit.]

D. [The following through paragraph X. below is largely repeated in Yoma 69a:]
   This last remark contradicts the body [of Mishnah]! For [Mishnah clearly
   says], They lay them down under their heads.

E. We must conclude then that priestly garments were indeed available for
   personal benefit.

F. [This interpretation of Mishnah is incorrect. Mishnah means that priest may
   fold the garments and lay them down] next to their heads [but not under their
   heads as a pillow].

G. Said R. Papa, [disagreeing with F], "May we infer from this that it is
   permissible to place also phylacteries next to one's head [while sleeping]
   without fearing that one will roll over on them?" [This would be absurd.]

H. [The authority of D-E responds that] it also follows logically [that Mishnah
   only allows the priest to lay his garments] next to his head [and not under
   it], for if you say Mishnah allows the priest to place the garment under his
   head, then it means that it is available for personal benefit. You then are
   exempting the priests from the prohibition against using fabric woven of
   diverse kinds [cf. Lev. 19:19. The High Priest's garments were made of flax
   and wool.]

I. [27B] [This last argument] is plausible for those who hold that the belt of
   the high priest [which is woven of diverse fabrics] is not the same as the
   belt of the ordinary priest [whose belt it would follow, is woven of a single
   fabric. Ordinary priests, on this view, have belts of a single fabric
   because they are subject to the law of diverse kinds.] But for those who say
   that the belt of the high priest is the same as the belt of the ordinary

priest [i.e., that all priests use belts made of both linen and wool], then
what is there to say in H? [The ordinary priest may use cloth woven of
diverse kinds just as the High Priest may.]

J. Now you might argue that putting on or wearing a garment woven of mixed
fibers is prohibited [to an ordinary priest], but spreading them out is
permitted [as D-E says]. For it is taught (Lev. 19:19), "It should not come
upon you," [meaning that you must not wear it], but you may spread it out
under you.

K. Indeed: the sages say, "It is forbidden [to the priest even to lie on such a
garment for just this reason], namely, lest a thread [of the garment] should
wrap around his body [such that he would have it upon him]."

L. And if you should [try to set aside this argument] by saying, "It does not
come on him directly [and so is not really upon him," lo, this has already
been rejected] for R. Simeon said R. Joshua b. Levi said R. Yose b. Saul
said in the name of the holy congregation of Jerusalem, "Even if one has ten
mats one upon the other and [only] the bottom one is of a forbidden mixture,
it is forbidden to sleep on [the whole pile. That is, even the most indirect
wearing of mixed kinds is prohibited.]"

M. We infer from this [that Mishnah must mean that the priests may lay the
garments only] next to their heads [but not under them, as F says.]

N. And if you insist, I say that [Mishnah's prohibition includes even] garments
that are not of diverse kinds [just to insure that no infringement occurs.]

O. R. Ashi said, "[The fear that a thread of mixed kinds might come upon the
priest while he sleeps on the garment is baseless,] since the priestly
garments were tightly woven. This we know because R. Huna the son of R.
Joshua said, '[Only] this stiff fabric of Naresh is permitted [for use in
making priestly garments].'"

X.

A. Come and hear: As for the priestly garments, it is forbidden to wear them
outside the Temple. But one may wear them within the Temple compound, both
when offerings are being made and when they are not being made. We conclude
from this that such garments are available [to the priests] for personal
benfit [Cf. IX. B].

B. But is it not true [that in fact they may wear the priestly garments] outside
the Temple? For is it not taught on Tannaitic authority, "On the twenty-
first day of the month [of Tevet] is the day of Mt. Gerizim, on which they do
not mourn. . . ."? [The story proceeds to tell how the Samaritans chose this
day to appeal to Alexander the Great to stop the rebuilding of the Temple in
Jerusalem. Simeon the Just went to meet Alexander to plead the priests'
cause. He did so wearing the priestly garments.]

C. This is related in Yoma [69a] from "The High Priest used to come" through
[the following interpretation]: "If you want I can argue that this was a
proper use for priestly garments [i.e., they may be worn outside the Temple];
or, if you like, I can argue [that this was an extraordinary case, and not a
precedent at all. It is like what is written in Ps. 119:126], 'It was time
to work for the Lord, so they violated the law [this one time for the greater
good].'"

XI

A. [Turning to Mishnah 1:1K-L] If one of them should have a nocturnal emission,
[he goes out proceeding along the passage that leads below the building. .
.]:

B. This supports the view of R. Yohanan who said, "The underground tunnels [of
the Temple] were not consecrated so that the priest who had a nocturnal
emission could be [safely] sent out of the two [holiest] precincts."

XII

A. [M. 1:1L-O goes on to say,] lamps flicker on this side and on that, [until he
reaches the immersion-room, and there was a fire there, and a privy in good
taste]:

B. R. Safra was once sitting on the privy when R. Abba came and coughed.
[Safra] said to him, "Come in!" [Abba waited.] When he came out, R. Abba
said to him, "If you have not become a goat you at least act like one. Have
we not taught, 'If you find [the door to the privy] locked, you can be sure
someone is inside [and should not yourself go in]'? Does it not follow that
you should surely not allow one to enter [if the privy is already
occupied]?"

C. But R. Safra [said, "Come in!" because he] thought that it would be dangerous [for Abba to wait], as it is taught, "R. Simeon b. Gamaliel says, 'Holding back feces causes dropsy. Holding back urine causes jaundice.'"

D. Rab said to his son Hiyya, and R. Hanina said to his son Rabbah, "Take care of your bodily needs at nightfall and at daybreak [when you are at home] rather than having to go a long way [to a privy in the middle of the day, thereby endangering your health]."

E. [The proper procedure in the privy is:] First sit and then uncover; first cover and then get up.

F. Also, one should rinse [one's cup] before drinking, then rinse it before putting it down. And when you are drinking water, pour some out before handing it to your disciples, as it is taught, "One should not drink water [from a cup] and then hand it to a disciple unless he has first poured some out."

G. [The reason is as follows:] It once happened that a certain [scholar] drank some water and without pouring any out, he handed [the cup] to his disciple. This disciple was fastidious and did not want to drink [from the unrinsed cup. Consequently,] he died of thirst.. At that time they said, "One should not drink water [from a cup] and then hand it to a disciple unless he has first poured some out."

H. Rav Ashi said, "Therefore, a disciple like this who pours water out of a cup [offered by his teacher] does not show disrespect."

I. Do not spit anything out in front of your teachers except for [the liquid that rises after eating] pumpkin and leek for [this liquid, if swallowed, burns] like a stream of molten lead.

XII

A. We taught there: The man in charge of the Temple Mount would go around to every watch, and lighted torches were [flaring] before him.

B. And to any watch which was not standing did [28A] the man in charge of the Temple Mount say, "Peace be with you."

C. [If] it was obvious that he was sleeping, he beats him with his staff.

D. And he had the right to burn his garment.

E.   They would say, "What is that noise in the courtyard?"

F.   [Others answered,] "It is the sound of a Levite being beaten and his clothes
     being burned, for he fell asleep at his post."

G.   R. Eliezer b. Jacob says, "Once they found my mother's brother asleep [at his
     post] and they burned his garments [=M. Middot 1:2]:

H.   Said R. Hiyya bar Abba, "When R. Yohanan came to this passage in Mishnah, he
     said as folows, 'Happy are these earlier generations who exacted punishment
     even for giving way to sleep. How much more so [must they have exacted
     punishment for transgressions] not caused by sleep!'"

I.   It is taught [elsewhere]: "Rabbi says, 'What is the proper path one should
     choose for oneself? One should love reproof, for as long as there is
     reproof, peace of mind comes into the world, goodness and blessing come to
     the world and evil flees from the world, as it is said (Prov. 24:25), 'Those
     who are reproved will be comforted. Good blessing shall come upon them.'"

J.   Some say that one should strengthen oneself in faith, as it is said (Psalms
     101:6), "My eyes are upon the faithful of the land so that they might sit
     with me . . ."

K.   Said R. Samuel ben Nahmani, said R. Yohanan, "Everyone who reproves his
     fellow for the sake of heaven gains a portion next to The Holy One Blessed be
     He, as it is said (Prov. 28:23), 'One who reproves a person [follows] after
     me' [or 'will find favor in the end'].

W.   "Furthermore, a thread of mercy shall be drawn around him, as it is said [in
     that same verse: 'He who reproves a man will in the end] find more favor
     than he who flatters.'"

XIV.

A.   [Turning to M. 1:1P: If] he found it locked, he knows that someone is there.
     . .:

B.   [Turning to M. 1:2A-B] "He who wants to take up [the ashes] from the altar
     gets up early and immerses before the superintendent comes by. . .:

C.   This seems to pose a contradiction. You said, He who wants to take up [the
     ashes] from the altar gets up early and immerses before the superintendent
     comes by. This implies that it does not depend on a lottery. But it is also

taught, <u>Let him who has immersed come and cast lots</u> [M. 1:2H]. This implies that it does depend on a lottery.

D. Said Abayye, "This is not difficult [to explain]. The first statement applies before the new regulation [was instituted calling for a lottery]; the later applies after the new regulation,

E. "for we learned, 'At first whoever wanted to take up the ashes would take them up. When volunteers become numerous, they would run up the ramp and whoever arrived first within four cubits won [the right to take up the ashes that morning].

F. "'If there was a tie, the superintendent would say to the [onlookers], 'Indicate [your choice]!' What would they put out? Either one finger or two fingers.

G. "'But they would not stick out their thumbs in the Temple compound.

H. "'<u>M'SH B</u>: two [priests] were running neck and neck up the ramp, and one pushed the other and broke his leg. When the court saw that matters were getting out of hand, they decreed that the assignment to take up ashes would be determined by lottery.'"

I. Raba said, "Both statements [cited in C reflect the situation] after this decree. It should be read this way, 'He who wants to come and be in the lottery [for taking up the ash], gets up early and immerses before the superintendent comes by.'"

Talmud systematically moves through M. 1:1's description of the Temple, finding Scriptural warrants, clarifying language and explaining Mishnah's rulings. On only three occasions are extraneous considerations introduced, all based on Mishnah Middot. Units VII–VIII comprise an aside on M. Middot 1:1. Although M. Middot is generally relevant to our theme, I cannot see why Talmud chooses to take up these materials just here. Unit X, which discusses the use of the priestly garb, is placed here on account of IX. Finally, XIII cites a long passage from M. Middot 1:2 to serve as an exordium to Talmud's discussion.

1:3-4

A. He took the key and opened the door and entered via the room of the hearth into the Temple courtyard.

B. And they entered after him with two lighted torches in their hands.

C. And they divided into two parties.

D. These go along the colonnade eastward, and those go along the colonnade westward.

E. They would go along and inspect [to make sure everything was in order], until they reach the place where they make the baked cakes.

F. These met up with those.

G. They said, "Is it in order"?

I. [The others respond,] "All is in order."

J. They had those who make the baked cakes begin to make baked cakes.

M. 1:3

A. He who had won [the right] to take up [the ash] from the altar [Lev. 6:3]—he will take up the ash from the altar.

B. And they said to him, "Be careful not to touch a utensil [the fire-shovel] before you sanctify your hands and your feet in the laver."

C. And lo, the fire-shovel is placed in the corner between the ramp and the altar, at the westward side of the ramp.

D. No one goes in with him, nor is there a light in his hand.

E. But he goes along by the light of the altar-fire.

F. They did not see him, [28B] nor did they hear a sound from him until they hear the noise of the wooden device which Ben Qatin made for the laver [M. Yoma 3:10].

G. And they say, "The time has come."

H. He sanctified his hands and feet with the laver.

I. He took the silver fire-shovel and went up to the top of the altar, and he cleared away the cinders from one side and the other, scooped up the innermost ashes, and came down.

J. He reached the pavement.

K. He turned his face northward [toward the altar].

L. He went along ten cubits to the east of the ramp.

M. He heaped up the cinders together on the pavement, three handbreadths from
the ramp,

N. the place in which they toss the crops of fowl, and the ashes of the
innermost altar and the candlestick.

M. 1:4

I.

A. [As regards M. 1:3D,] was there really a colonnade in the courtyard?

B. Was it not taught, "R. Eliezer ben Jacob says, 'From where [in Scripture] do
we know that they may not build a colonnade in the courtyard?

C. "'[We know this from Deut. 16:21 which says,] 'You may plant no asherah; you
may plant no tree next to the altar of the Lord your God.' Can this mean
simply that you may plant no asherah and you may plant no tree next to the
altar of the Lord your God? [No, it means also that you may not build next to
the altar anything that looks like a tree, i.e., a colonnade.]'"

D. Said Rav Hisda, "[Although one may not build a colonade next to the altar,
one may have] a colonnade [that is part] of the building."

II.

A. [Turning to M. 1:3E:] They would go along and inspect until they reached the
place where they make the baked cakes:

B. Is this to say that the baked cakes were the first things offered?

C. [No,] for is it not taught [on Tannaitic authority]: "From where [in
Scripture] do we learn that nothing precedes the daily [animal] sacrifice in
the morning? From [Lev. 6:5,] which says, 'Arrange the burnt-offering on
it.'"

D. And said Rabbah, "[When Scripture specifies] the burnt-offering, [this is
meant to indicate that] it is the first offering [of the day, preceeding even
the bread]."

E.   Said R. Judah, "[Actually the reference in Mishnah is not to the wafers at
     all, but only to the place in which they] would heat the water for making the
     dough."

     The   authorities of Talmud find apparent contradictions in Scripture to M.
1:3D (unit I) and M. 1:3E (unit II).   Both apparent contradictions are resolved.

CHAPTER TEN

BAVLI TAMID CHAPTER TWO

2:1-5

A. His brothers saw that he came down, and they came running.

B. They hastened and sanctified their hands and their feet from the laver.

C. They took the shovels and the rakes and went up to the top of the altar.

D. The limbs and the fat pieces which had not been consumed the preceding night they raked to the sides of the altar.

E. If the sides did not hold them, they arranged them on the circuit by the ramp.

M. 2:1

A. They began heaping up ashes on the apple [ash-pile].

B. And the apple was in the middle of the altar.

C. Sometimes there were three hundred kors [of ashes].

D. And at festivals they did not clear away the ashes,

E. for they are an ornament to the altar.

F. [29A] The priest never through neglect failed to remove the ashes.

M. 2:2

A. They began heaping up the twigs to prepare the altar-fire.

B. And are all sorts of wood valid for the altar-fire?

C. Yes.

D. All sorts of wood are valid for the altar fire,

E. except for olive-wood and wood of the vine.

F. But with these were they used [to light the fire]: boughs (1) of the fig-tree, or (2) of the walnut-tree, or (3) of oleaster-wood.

M. 2:3

A. He arranged the altar-fire, the larger one on the east side, with its open side [at which side it was tended] facing east.

B.   And the tips of the inner twigs were touching the apple.

C.   And there was a space between the twigs, through which they set fire to the
     kindling-wood.

M. 2:4

A.   They selected from there fine pieces of fig-wood [= M. 2:3Fl] [with which]
     to arrange the second altar-fire, [the one] for the incense,

B.   toward the south-western corner, four cubits to the north of the corner.

C.   [On weekdays, they took] sufficient [wood to produce] an amount of five seahs
     of cinders, and on the Sabbath, sufficient for an amount of eight seahs of
     cinders.

D.   For there [A] did they place the two dishes of frankincense which accompany
     the show-bread.

E.   The limbs and pieces of fat which had not been consumed the preceding evening
     they put back on the altar-fire.

F.   They kindled the two altar-fires.

G.   And they came down.

H.   And they went to the office made of hewn stone.

M. 2:5

I.

A.   Said Raba, "[The claim in M. 2:2C that there were 300 kor of ashes on the
     altar] is an exaggeration."

B.   [As for M. 3:4B:] They gave [the lamb which was to be] the daily whole-
     offering a drink from a golden cup—said Raba, "It is an exaggeration."

C.   Said R. Ammi, "The Pentateuch uses hyperbole; the prophets use hyperbole and
     the sages use hyperbole:

D.   "The Torah uses hyperbole, for it says (Deut. 1:28), 'Great cities fortified
     to the heavens.' Do you think this means really to the heavens? It is an
     exaggeration.

E.   "The sages use hyperbole, as in the cases we just mentioned, i.e., the pile
     of ashes, and also in They gave [the lamb which was to be] the daily whole-
     offering a drink from a golden cup [M. 3:4B].

F. "The prophets use hyperbole, as it says [in 1 Kings 1:40], 'and all the people played their flutes . . . and the earth opened up due to the noise.'"

G. Said R. Yannai b. Nahmani, said Samuel, "The sages used hyperbole in three places, and these are they: 1) regarding the heap of ashes, 2) regarding the vine, and 3) regarding the veil."

H. This excludes Raba's example, as we learned, "[As regards:] They gave [the lamb which was to be] the daily whole-offering a drink from a golden cup-- Raba said, 'This is an exaggeration!'"

I. This shows us that the former [three, alluded to by Yannai,] are exaggerations while this one is not [i.e., they actually used gold cups to give the animals drink].

J. [The reason is that] they do not scrimp in a place of wealth [i.e., the Temple].

K. [We shall now list the three examples of exaggeration enumerated by Yannai in G:] 1) The pile of ash--as we have just stated [i.e., the claim that there were 300 kor of ashes a day].

L. 2) The vine--it is taught [in M. Mid. 3:8]: A golden vine was standing at the entrance of the sanctuary, trained over posts. Whoever donates a leaf [29B] or a berry or a cluster brings it and hangs it on it.

M. Said R. Eleazar ben Sadoq, "It once happened that three hundred priests were appointed to remove it [because it was so heavy. This is the exaggeration.]"

N. 3) The veil--as we teach [in Shek. 12b], "Rabban Simeon ben Gamaliel says in the name of R. Simeon the associate, 'The thickness of the veil was a handbreadth. It was woven on 72 strands, with 24 threads per strand. It was 40 cubits [about 60 feet] long and 20 cubits wide. It was made by 82 young maidens. Two were made each year and it took 300 priests to immerse it.'" [These are all exaggerations.]

II.

A. [Turning to Mishnah 2:3:] They began heaping up the twigs to prepare the altar fire [. . .except for olive-wood and wood of the vine]:

B. Why is this so?

C.   R. Papa said, "Because these are knotty [and so burn poorly]."

D.   R. Aha bar Jacob said, "Because [of their importance for human] settlement
     in the land of Israel." [That is, they avoided using these woods lest they
     become extinct.]

E.   They responded [in favor of R. Papa by citing Lev. 1:8], "On the wood that is
     on the fire." [This means] any wood that is readily combustible. What are
     these? Thin spits which do not form knots [which grow into the wood].

F.   [The following also supports Papa's view that knotty wood is not used on the
     altar:] [B. adds: Reverting to M. 2:3B-E:] Are all [sorts of] wood valid for
     the altar-fire? [. . .] All [sorts of] wood are valid except for olive-wood
     and wood of the vine [since these are prone to form knots].

G.   Indeed, they were most accustomed [to using these]: boughs of fig trees, nut
     trees and oil trees.

H.   R. Eliezer adds [to the list of non-usable wood] also mayish-wood, and
     oak, and palm, and carob, and sycamore.

I.   [R. Eliezer's additions] make sense if you hold [that we disqualify wood] if
     it is knotty [= C].

J.   [On this view, Eliezer and F] disagree [only about] the following: [Eliezer]
     holds that [even though Mayish, oak, palm, etc.] do not form knots on the
     inside, we do not bring them because they form knots on the surface and [F]
     holds that since they do not form knots on the inside, we bring them even
     though they do not form knots on the surface.

K.   But if you hold [that we disqualify wood] because of its importance for the
     settlement of the Land of Israel [D, Eliezer's additions are a problem]. For
     does not the palm have importance for the settlement of the land of Israel?
     [Yet he allows it to be burned.]

L.   I can say to you [i.e. to Aha] further, "According to your reasoning, fig
     trees [also should be disqualified], for are they not important for the
     settlement of the Land? [Yet everyone, = F, agrees they may be used. It
     thus must be that wood is deemed unfit for the altar because it forms knots
     as Papa says, not because it is necessary for the settlement of the Land, as
     Aha says.]" How can you respond to that?

M. [Aha respondsd as follows:] Just as [G] allows [wood from] fig trees which do
    not produce fruit, so also, [it allows wood from] palm trees which do not
    produce fruit. [Aha now says his point is that wood is prohibited if it is
    important for the settlement of the Land and it bears fruit. Since these do
    not bear fruit, they are not disqualified, even though they are important for
    settling the Land.]

N. But are there fig trees that do not produce fruit?

O. Yes, as Rahabah [has said], for Rahabah said, "Bring white fig trees [30A]
    and rub them with a strap of fig tree bark on which [fig] seed is smeared [to
    impregnate the wood]. Plant them in soil washed by the sea. They produce a
    stem but they do not produce fruit. And [the stems are so large and heavy]
    that no bridge can bear more than three [at one time]."

III.

A. [Turning to M. 2:4,] He arranged the altar-fire, the larger one on the east
    side, with its open end facing east. . . .":

B. What is the reason [for having the open end facing east]?

C. Rav Huna and Rav Hisda [disagree]. One says, "So that the wind can blow into
    the fire." The other says, "So that they can ignite the kindling from
    there."

D. They reject [the second opinion on the basis of M. 2:4C, which states], "And
    there was a space between the twigs, through which they set fire to the
    kindling wood." [So a special opening was not necessary.]

E. [The other] can respond [to D as follows, "They set fire to the kindling]
    from several places, [so they need an opening at the east as well as the
    spaces between the twigs]."

Unit I takes up M. 2:2 and its clearly exaggerated numbers. It shows that
Mishnah uses exaggerations in other cases as well. Unit II turns to the next
Mishnaic pericope, M. 2:3. The interest here is to adduce the logic which
excludes certain types of wood from the altar. Unit III, finally, turns to M.
2:4, attempting to account for the orientation of the altar fire.

CHAPTER ELEVEN

BAVLI TAMID CHAPTER THREE

3:1-9

A.   The superintendent said to them, "Come and cast lots [to determine] (1) who executes the act of slaughter, (2) who tosses the blood, (3) who removes the ashes of the inner altar, (4) who removes the ashes of the candlestick, (5) who carries up the limbs to the ramp:

B.   "the head, (2) the [right] hind-leg, (3) the two fore-legs, (4) the rump, and (5) the [left] hind-leg, (6) the breast, (7) the neck, (8) the two flanks, (9) the innards, (10) the fine flour, (11) the cakes, (12) the wine."

C.   They drew lots.

D.   Whoever won won.

M. 3:1

A.   The superintendent said to them, "Go and see whether the time for carrying out the act of slaughter has come."

B.   If it had come, the one who sees it says, "It is daylight."

C.   Matya b. Samuel says, "[He who sees it says,] 'The whole eastern horizon is light.'

D.   "'Up to Hebron'?

E.   "And he says, 'Yes.'"

M. 3:2

A.   He said to them, "Go and bring a lamb from the lamb-office."

B.   Now lo, the lamb-office was located at the north-western corner.

C.   And there were four offices there:

(1) one was the lamb-office;

(2) and one was the seal-office;

(3) and one was the hearth-office;

(4) and one was the office in which they would prepare the show-bread.

M. 3:3

-149-

A.   They went into the office for utensils and brought out from there ninety-
     three silver and gold utensils.

B.   They gave [the lamb which was to be] the daily whole-offering a drink from a
     golden [30B] cup.

C.   Even though it was inspected the preceding night, they inspect it again by
     the light of the torches.

                              M. 3:4

A.   He who had won [the right to carry out the rite] of the daily burnt-offering
     drags it along down to the shambles, and those who had won the right to offer
     up the limbs go after him.

B.   The shambles was located at the north of the altar, and on it were eight
     short pillars, and square blocks of cedar-wood were on them.

C.   And iron hooks were set into them.

D.   And there were three rows [of hooks] on each one [block], on which they would
     suspend [the slaughtered beasts].

E.   And they flay them on marble tables between the pillars.

                              M. 3:5

A.   Those who had won the right to remove the ashes of the inner altar and of the
     candlestick would go first,

B.   with four utensils in their hand, the ash-bin, the oil-jar, and two keys.

C.   The ash-bin is like a large golden three-qab measure. It holds two and half
     qabs.

D.   The oil-jar is like a large golden flagon.

E.   The two keys--one goes down [into the lock] as far as its armpit, and one
     opens [the door] forthwith.

                              M. 3:6

A.   He came to the northern door.

B.   And the great gate had two [such] doors, one at the north, and one at the
     south.

C. Into that at the south no man ever entered. And this is expressly stated
    concerning it by Ezekiel: And the Lord said to me, This gate shall be shut,
    it shall not be opened, neither shall any man enter in by it, for the Lord,
    the God of Israel, hath entered in by it: therefore it shall be shut (Ez.
    44:2).

D. He took the key and opened the door.

E. He went into the cell, and from the cell into the hekhal, until he came to
    the great gate.

F. He came to the great gate.

G. He removed the bolt and the locks and opened it up.

H. The one who was going to execute the act of slaughter did not perform the
    fact of slaughter until he heard the sound of the great gate opening.

                              M. 3:7

A. (1) From Jericho did they hear the sound of the great gate opening.

B. (2) From Jericho did they hear the sound of the shovel [M. 5:6].

C. [Following B. and V.:] (3) From Jericho did they hear the sound of Ben Arza
    [V. has Ben Aryeh] clashing the cymbals.

D. (4) From Jericho did they hear the sound of the flute.

E. (5) From Jericho did they hear the sound of the Gabini, the crier.

F. (6) From Jericho did they hear the sound of the wooden device which Ben Qatin
    made for the laver.

G. (7) From Jericho did they hear the sound of the singing.

H. (8) From Jericho did they hear the sound of the shofar.

I. There are those who say, "Also the voice of the high priest when he made
    mention of the divine name on the Day of Atonement."

J. (9) From Jericho did they smell the scent of the compounding of the incense,

K. [Following B. and V.] Said R. Eleazar b. Diglai, "My father had goats in the
    villages of Mikhwar. And they sneezed from the smell of the compounding of
    the incense."

                              M. 3:8

A. He who had won the right to collect the ash of the inner altar entered in.

B. And he took the ash-bin, put it down before him, and scooped up ashes with both hands and put them into it.

C. And at the end he swept the rest into it.

D. And he left it and went out.

E. He who had won the right to clean the candlestick entered, and [if] he found the two eastern lights flickering, he cleaned the rest and left those flickering in their place.

F. [If] he found that they had gone out, he cleaned them and lit them from those which were [yet] flickering.

H. A stone was before the candlestick, and on it were three steps, on which the priest stands and fixes up the lamps.

I. And he left the oil-jar on the second step and went out.

M. 3:9

4:1-3

A. They did not [wholly] bind up the lamb, but [only] tied it[s foreleg and hindleg].

B. Those who had won [the privilege of taking] the limbs take hold of it.

C. And thus was the manner of tying it:

D. its head to the south [toward the altar], and its face to the west [toward the heikhal].

E. He who effects the act of slaughter stands in the east with his face to the west.

F. And that [daily whole-offering] of the dawn was slaughtered at the northwestern corner, at the second ring.

G. That [daily whole-offering] of twilight was slaughtered at the northeastern corner [of the altar], at the second ring.

H. The slaughterer slaughtered.

I. The one who receives the blood received the blood.

J. He came to the northeastern corner.

K. He tosses [the blood] in a northeasterly direction,

L. [Then he came] to the southwestern corner.

M. He tosses [the blood] in a southwesterly direction,

N. The residue of the blood did he pour out on the southern base [of the altar].

M. 4:1

A. [31A] He [who slaughtered the daily whole-offering] did not break the hindleg. But he pierces it at the knee-joint and hangs it up therewith.

B. He did flay it downward, until he reached the breast.

C. [When] he reached the breast, he cut off the head and gave it to him who had won it.

-153-

D. He cut off the shanks and gave them to him who had won them.

E. He stripped off the hide.

F. He cut open the heart and removed its blood.

G. He cut off the fore-legs and gave them to him who had won them.

H. He came up to the right hind-leg, cut it off, and gave it to him who had won it, and the two testicles with it.

I. He cut it [the carcass] open, so that all of it was open before him.

J. He took the fat and put it at the place at which the head had been cut off above.

K. He took the innards and gave them to him who had won them, for the purpose of washing them.

L. And as to the stomach: they wash it in the swilling-room, so much as was required.

M. And as to the innards: they wash them three times at the very least, on the marble tables which are between the pillars.

M. 4:2

A. He took the knife and separated the lungs from the liver, and the lobe of the liver from the liver.

B. But he did not move it from its place.

C. He pierced the breast and gave it to him who had won it.

D. He proceeded to the right flank and did cut it down-wards to the backbone—

E. but he did not touch the backbone—

F. until he reached the two thin ribs.

G. He cut it off and gave it to him who had won it, with the liver suspended from it.

H. He came to the neck, and left with it two ribs on this side and two ribs on that side.

I. He cut it off and gave it to him who had won it, with the windpipe, heart, and lungs hanging from it.

J. He came to the left flank and left with it two thin ribs above and two thin ribs below.

K. And so did he leave them on the other side.

L. It turns out that he left on both of them two each above and two each below.

M. He cut it off and gave it to him who had won it, and the backbone with it, and the spleen hanging from it.

N. This was the larger part, but that of the right side do they call the larger part, for the liver is suspended on it.

O. He came to the rump, cut it off, and gave it to him who had won it, with the fat tail, and the lobe of the liver, and the two kidneys with it.

P. He took the left hind-leg, [B. and V. add:] cut it off, and gave it to him who had won it.

Q. All of them turned out to be standing in a row, and the limbs in their hands:

(1) [31B] the first, with the head and a hindleg, the head in his right hand, with its muzzle along his arm, and its horns in his fingers, and the place at which it was slaughtered turned upwards, and the fat set on top of it [that place], and the right hind-leg in his left hand, and the flayed end outermost;

(2) the second, with the two fore-legs, that of the right hand in his right hand, and that of the left in his left, with the flayed end outermost;

(3) the third, with the rump and the [other] hind-leg, the rump in his right hand, and the fat-tail hanging down between his fingers, and the lobe of the liver and the two kidneys with it, the left hind-leg in his left hand, with the flayed end outermost;

(4) the fourth, with the breast and the neck, the breast in his right hand, and the neck in his left, and with its ribs between his fingers;

(5) the fifth with the two flanks, that of the right in his right hand, that of the left in his left, with the flayed ends outwards;

(6) the sixth, with the innards put in a dish, and the shanks on top of them, above;

(7) the seventh, with the fine flour;

(8) the eighth, with the baked cakes;

(9) the ninth, with the wine.

R. <u>They went and put them on the lower half of the ramp, on the west side of</u>
<u>it.</u>

S. <u>And they salted them [the limbs and meal-offering].</u>

T. <u>Then they came down and came to the office of hewn stone to recite the</u>
<u>Shema.</u>

M. 4:3

I.

A. <u>They did not wholly bind up the lamb, but only tied (m'qydym) its [forelegs</u>
<u>and hindlegs...]</u>[M. 4:1A]:

B. [A Tanna] taught, "[This means they tied up] its forelegs and hindlegs as in
the binding ['qydt] of Isaac the son of Abraham."

II.

A. <u>They did not [wholly] bind up the lamb...</u>":

B. What is the reason?

   C. R. Huna and R. Hisda [disagreed]. One says, "So as not to show
   disrespect to holy things [by bruising the animal more than necessary]." The
   other says, "So as not to follow pagan practice."

D. What is the practical difference?

E. The practical difference occurs [if the priest proposed wholly to bind the
animal] with silk strands. [This is permitted by the first opinion since
silk does not cause bruises, but is prohibited by the second because it still
follows pagan practice.]

F. The same is true [if he binds it with] strands of gold.

III.

A. We teach elsewhere: <u>There were thirteen tables in the sanctuary: eight</u>
<u>marble ones were in the slaughter area. On these they washed the innards.</u>
<u>Two were on the west side of the ramp; one of the marble and one of silver.</u>
<u>On the marble one they placed the [severed] limbs and on the silver one they</u>
<u>put the vessels of service. In the forecourt there were two on the inner</u>
<u>side by the sanctuary door: one of silver and one of gold. They placed the</u>
<u>showbread on the silver one when they were bringing it in and they placed it</u>

on the golden one when they were taking it out because you always treat holy

things with increasing [respect] and never with diminished [respect]. And

one golden table was inside [the sanctuary] on which the showbread always

rested [= M. Sheqalim 6:4]:

B. Now [we have said] that you never scrimp in a place of wealth [cf. M. 2:1I–

J]. Why then [are some of the tables] made of marble? Let them all be

silver! or let them all be gold! [To do less is to show disrespect to the

altar.]

C. Said R. Hinnena in the name of R. Assi, and R. Assi said in the name of R.

Samuel b. Rav Isaac, "[They are made of marble] because [if they were metal]

they would sear [the meat placed on them]."

IV.

A. And that [daily whole-offering] of the dawn was slaughtered at the

northeastern [M. has northwestern] corner, at the second ring.[M. 4:1F]:

B. What is the scriptural basis for this location?

C. Said Rav Hisda, "Scripture says (Nu. 28:3), "Two per day." [This means each

is to be slaughtered] toward [the place where] day [begins, i.e., the

northeast].

D. Along the same lines it is taught, "'Two per day'. This means toward [the

place where] day [begins]."

E. You say this [phrase] means toward [the northeast]. But perhaps it means

[not a direction, but that] the obligation occurs each day.

F. [We know this is not so because we derive this obligation from elsewhere,

namely, Nu. 28:4:] For when Scripture says, "Prepare the one lamb in the

morning and the other lamb in the evening," lo, the obligation of each day is

mentioned. What do I learn then from the phrase "two per day" [in Numbers

28:3? I learn that they are to be slaughtered] toward [the place] where day

begins [i.e., the northeast corner.]

G. How was this done?

H. The daily whole-offering of the dawn was slaughtered at the northwest corner

at the second ring, and that of the evening was slaughtered on the northeast

corner at the second ring. [M.4:1F–G]

V.

A. Ten questions did Alexander [the Great] of Macedonia ask the elders of the
   south:

B. He said to them [32A], "Is it farther from east to west or from heaven to
   earth?"

C. They said, "From east to west. For you know that when the sun is in the east
   everyone can look at it, and when the sun is in the west everyone can look at
   it, but when it is in the center [i.e., at noon], no one can look at it
   [because it is too close]."

D. The sages say, "Both distances are equal, as it is said (Psalms 103:11, 12),
   'As the heavens are high above the earth . . . as the distance from east to
   west.' Now if one were greater, let both [verses] use the greater distance!"
   [Since both examples are used, they must be the same.]

E. [And according to their view,] why is it that no one can look at the sun when
   it is in the center of the sky?

F. Because it stands alone, with nothing obstructing [its brilliance].

F. [The second question was:] "Were the heavens created first, or the earth?"

G. They said, "The heavens were created first, as it says (Gen. 1:1), 'When God
   began to create the heavens and the earth.'"

H. [The third question] he asked was, "Was light created first, or darkness?"

I. They said, "There is no answer to that."

J. Let them say, "Darkness was created first, for it is written (Gen. 1:2),
   'The earth was unformed and void, and darkness . . .' and later 'And God
   said, 'Let there be light' and light was.'"

K. [They did not answer this way because they began to] think: What if he
   begins to ask about what is above and what is below, what is before and what
   is after? [Since we cannot discuss such questions, we had best stop
   answering altogether.]

L. If so, then they should not have answered his question about the heavens [or
   the earth either].

M. [They answered this question because] they thought he just happened upon that
   question. But when they saw that he was pursuing that line of questions,

they thought: we will not answer any more lest he begin to ask about what is above and what is below, what is before and what is after.

N. [The fourth question] he asked was, "Who are called wise?"

O. They said, "Who is wise? He who sees what is about to happen."

P. [The fifth question] he asked was, "Who is called mighty?"

Q. They said, "Who is mighty? He who conquers his lusts."

R. [The sixth question] he asked was, "Who is called rich?"

S. They said, "Who is rich? He who is happy with his lot."

T. [The seventh question] he asked was, "What should one do to live?"

U. They said, "He should kill himself [i.e., be humble, so as to gain eternal life]."

V. [The eighth question] he asked was, "And what should one do to die?"

W. They said, "He should cause himself to live [i.e., indulge himself and so merit eternal death].

X. [The ninth question] he asked was, "What can one do to be accepted among people?"

Y. They said, "Let him hate government and sovereignty."

Z. He said, "[In this] my answer is better than yours. [I say] 'Let him love government and sovereignty and do favors for people.'"

AA. [The tenth question] he asked was, "Is it better to live in the sea or on dry land?"

BB. They answered, "It is better to live on dry land. For those who set out to sea never have peace of mind until they return to land."

CC. He asked them, "Who is the wisest among you?"

DD. They said, "We are all alike in that for each question you posed we answered in one accord."

EE. He said to them, "Why do you resist me [by keeping to your own religion]?"

FF. They said, "[Because in you] Satan is victorious [i.e., your ascendency of the moment is due only to the power of Satan]."

GG. He said to them, "Lo, I shall have you all killed by royal decree!"

HH. They said to him, "Authority is in the hand of the king, and it does not befit a king to lie." [They were ready to obey.]

II. Thereupon he dressed them in purple garments, and placed chains of gold
around their necks [as a sign of respect].

JJ. He said to them, "I want to go to a city in Africa."

KK. They said to him, "You will be unable to go because the Mountains of Darkness
block [the way]."

LL. He said to them, "That is not enough to stop me. [Besides] is this what I am
asking you? Rather [I want you to tell me] what I need to do [to get
there]."

MM. They said to him, "Get some Libyan donkeys that can travel in the dark and
get some coils of rope. Tie [the rope] along the sides [of the route] so
that when you return you will be guided by them and arrive at your
destination."

NN. He did so. He traveled until he came to a place which was [inhabited only]
by women. He wanted to wage war against them. They said to him, "If you
kill us, people will say, 'He kills women!' If we kill you, they will say,
'He was a king that women could kill.'"

OO. He said to them, "Bring me some bread." They brought him bread of gold on a
table of gold. [32B] He said to them, "Can a person eat bread of gold?"
They said, "Seeing that you want [real] bread, do you not have any edible
bread in your own place such that you needed to set out and travel here?"
When he left, he had inscribed over the gate of the city: "I, Alexander of
Macedonia, was a fool until I came to this women's city in Africa and learned
a lesson from these women."

PP. As he was traveling, he sat by a certain well and [began] to eat bread. He
had some salted fish and as he was washing off [the salt], a [pleasing] odor
arose. He said, "From this we [can] deduce that the well comes from the
Garden of Eden."

QQ. Some say, "He took some water from it and washed his face [and then noticed
the aroma]."

RR. Some say, "He drew all of the water out until he reached the gates of the
Garden of Eden. He shouted, 'Open the gates!' They said [quoting Ps.
118:20], 'This is the gate of the Lord.' He said to them, 'I also am a king;

I too am important. Give me something.' They gave him an eyeball. He went

and weighed all his silver and gold against it, but they were not [heavy

enough] to outweigh it. He said to the rabbis, 'What is this [strange

eyeball]?' They said, 'It is the eyeball of all flesh and blood, which is

never satisfied.' He said to them, 'How do I know that this is so?' [In

response,] they took some dirt and covered it [as a symbolic burial].

Immediately it was outweighed. [This is in accordance with] what is written

(Prov. 27:20), 'As Death and Destruction are never satisfied, so the eyes of

people are never satisfied.'" [The Rabbis' act shows that people's desires

are quieted only at death.]

VI

A.   A Tanna of the School of Eliahu said, "Hell is above the skies."

B.   But others say it is beyond the Mountains of Darkness.

VII

A.   A Tanna of the School of Hiyya said, "Everyone who studies the Torah at night

has the Holy Presence with him as it is said (Lam. 2:12), 'Arise, cry out in

the night at the beginning of the watch. Pour out your heart like water

before the Lord.'"

B.   Said R. Eliezer b. Azariah, "Serious students increase peace in the world, as

it is said (Isaiah 104:13), 'All your children are students of God['s ways],

great shall be the peace of these children.'"

Mishnah provides a detailed exposition of how the daily burnt-offering is

offered.   Talmud discusses only the first portion of this description.   I-II

clarify and justify M. 4:1A.   III asks about the Temple furniture, a topic not

explicitly raised by M., but one inherent in its discussion.   IV finds a

Scriptural basis for M. 4:1F. V and VI have no discernable relation in theme or

substance to the Mishnah-passage, unless the first question, dealing with the

distance between east and west is placed here because of IV's interest. Unit VII

supplies an inspiring conclusion to the Talmud's reflections on M. Tamid.

CHAPTER THIRTEEN

BAVLI TAMID CHAPTER FIVE

5:1-6

A. The superintendent said to them, "Say one blessing."

B. They said a blessing, pronounced the Ten Commandments, the Shema [Hear O
Israel (Deut. 6:4-9)], And it shall come to pass if you shall hearken (Deut.
11:13-21), and And the Lord spoke to Moses (Num. 15:37-41).

C. They blessed the people with three blessings: True and sure, 'Abodah, and
the blessing of priests.

D. And on the Sabbath they add a blessing for the outgoing priestly watch.

M. 5:1

A. [The superintendent] said to them, "Those who are new to [the preparation of]
the incense, come and cast lots."

B. They cast lots.

C. Whoever won won.

D. "Those who are new with those who have had a chance [compare Song of Songs
7:14], come and cast lots on who will bring up the limbs from the ramp to the
altar."

E. R. Eliezer b. Jacob says, "He who brings up the limbs to the ramp [without
another lottery] is the one who brings them up onto the altar."

M. 5:2

A. They handed them [who had no assignment] to the ministers.

B. They did remove their clothing from them.

C. And they left them only their underpants alone.

D. And there were wall-niches there, on which were written [the names] of the
various pieces of clothing.

M. 5:3

A.   He who won [the right to offer] the incense did take the spoon.

B.   And the spoon was like a large gold three-qab measure, holding three qabs.

C.   And the dish was in it, [33A] full and heaped up with incense.

D.   And it had a cover.

E.   And there was a kind of covering on it.

                              M. 5:4

A.   He who won [the right to the ashes with] the firepan took the silver firepan
     and went up to the top of the altar and cleared away the cinders in either
     side and scooped up [ashes with the firepan].

B.   He came down and emptied them out into that [firepan] of gold.

C.   About a qab of cinders scattered from it, and he swept them out into the
     water-channel.

D.   And on the Sabbath he covered over them with a psykter.

E.   And a psykter was a large utensil, holding a letekh, and two chains were on
     it, one with which he pulled to lower it, and one with which it was held firm
     from above, so that it should not roll.

F.   And three purposes did it serve: (1) they turn it over on top of cinders;
     and (2) on a creeping thing on the Sabbath; and (3) they lower the ashes from
     on the altar with it.

                              M. 5:5

A.   [When] they reached the area between the porch and the altar, one man took
     the shovel and tosses it between the porch and the altar.

B.   No one in Jerusalem hears the voice of his fellow on account of the noise of
     the shovel.

C.   And three purposes did it serve: (1) a priest who hears it sound knows that
     his brethren the priests enter in to prostrate themselves, and he then runs
     and comes along; (2) and a son of a Levite who hears its noise knows that his
     brethren, the Levites, enter to say their song, and he then runs and comes
     along: (3) and the head of the priestly watch then had the unclean people
     stand at the eastern gate.

                              M. 5:6

6:1-3

A. They [the priests who were in charge of the incense and of removing the ashes] began to go up onto the steps of the porch.

B. Those who had won [the right to remove] the ashes of the inner altar and the candlestick went before them [= M. 3:6A].

C. He who had won [the right to clean] the ashes of the inner altar went in and took the basket [left at M. 3:9] and prostrated himself and went out.

D. He who had won [the right to remove] the ashes of the candlestick entered in.

E. And [if] he found the two eastern-most lamps still flicking, he clears out the eastern one and leaves the western one flickering,

F. for from it did he kindle the candlestick at twilight.

G. [If] he found that it had gone out, he cleaned it out and kindled it from the altar of the whole-offering [M. 3:9E-F].

H. He took the oil-jar from the second step [M. 3:9I] and prostrated himself and went him.

M. 6:1

A. He who had won [the right to make use of] the firepan heaped up the cinders on the [inner] altar and tamped them down with the back of the firepan and prostrated himself and went out.

M. 6:2

A. He who had won [the right to prepare] the incense did take the dish from the middle of the ladle and gave it [the ladle] to his friend or his relative.

B. [If] it had spilled [from the firepan] into it [the ladle], he put it into his two hands.

C. And they instruct him: "Be careful not to begin in front of you lest you be burned."

D. He began to tamp down and come out.

E. The one who was to offer the incense did not offer the incense until the superintendent said to him, "Offer the incense."

F. If he was a high priest, the superintendent says, "My lord, high priest, offer the incense."

G. The people departed, and he offered the incense and prostrated himself and went out.

M. 6:3

CHAPTER FIFTEEN

BAVLI TAMID CHAPTER SEVEN

7:1-4

A. [33B] When the high priest enters to prostrate himself, three [priests] support him: one by the right hand, one by the left, and one by the precious stones [on the shoulder-pieces of the ephod, Ex. 28:9].

B. And as soon as the superintendent heard the sound of the feet of the high priest, that he goes out [of the heikhal], he raised the curtain for him.

C. He went in and prostrated himself and went out.

D. And his brethren the priests went in and prostrated themselves and went out.

M. 7:1

A. They [the priests who had participated] came and stood on the steps of the porch.

B. They who were first [the one who removed the ashes of the inner altar, and the one who cleaned up the candlestick, the one who carried the shovel and the one who offered the incense and his associate] took up a position at the south of their brethren, the priests.

C. And five utensils were in their hand: (1) the ash-bin in the hand of one, and (2) the oil-jar in the hand of one, and (3) the fire-shovel in the hand of one, and (4) the [incense] dish in the hand of one, and (5) the ladle and its cover [M. 5:4] in the hand of one.

D. They said one [priestly] blessing for the people (Num. 6:24-26).

E. But: In the provinces they say it as three blessings, and in the sanctuary, as one blessing.

F. In the sanctuary they would pronounce the [divine] name as it is written, and in the provinces, by an epithet.

G. In the provinces the priests raise up the palms of their hands as high as their shoulders, and in the sanctuary, over their heads,

H. except for the high priest, who does not raise his hands higher than the frontlet.

I. R. Judah says, "Even the high priest raises his hands above the frontlet,

J. "since it is said, 'And Aaron lifted up his hands towards the people and
    blessed them' (Lev. 9:22)" [M. Sot. 7:6].

                                    M. 7:2

A. When the high priest wants to burn the offerings, he would go up on the ramp,
    with the prefect at his right.

B. [When] he reached the half way point of the ramp, the prefect took him by the
    right hand and led him up.

C. The first [of the nine priests, M. 4:3] handed him the head and the hind-leg,
    and he laid his hands on them and tossed them [into the altar-fire].

D. The second handed over to the first the two fore-legs. He gives them to the
    high priest. And he laid his hands on them and tossed them [into the altar-
    fire].

E. The second departed, going on his way.

F. And so did they hand over to him all the rest of the limbs, and he lays his
    hands on them, and tosses them [into the altar-fires].

G. And when he wants, he lays on his hands, but others throw [the pieces into
    the fire].

H. He comes then to walk around the altar [toward the right, to the southwestern
    corner].

I. From what point does he begin?

J. From the southeastern corner, then northeastern one, northwestern, and
    southwestern [see M. Zeb. 5:3].

K. They gave him wine to pour out.

L. The prefect stands at the corner, with a flag in his hand, and two priests
    stand at the table of the fat pieces, with two silver trumpets in their
    hands.

M. They sounded a prolonged sound (tq'), a wavering sound, and a prolonged
    sound.

N. They came and stood near Ben Arza, one on his right, one on his left.

O. He stopped down to pour out the wine, and the prefect waved the flag, and Ben
    Arza dashed the cymbal, and the Levites broke out in song.

P. [When] they reached a break [in the singing], they sounded a prolonged sound,
    and the people prostrated themselves.

Q. At every break [in the singing] was a prolonged blast, and at every prolonged
    blast, a prostration.

R. This is the order of the daily whole-offering in the liturgy of the house of
    our God. May it be [his] will that it be rebuilt, soon, in our own days.
    Amen.

M. 7:3

A. The singing which the Levites did sing in the sanctuary:

B. On the first day they did sing, The earth is the Lord's and the fulness
    thereof, the world and they who live therein (Ps. 24).

C. On the second day they did sing, Great is the Lord and highly to be praised
    in the city of our God, even upon his holy hill (Ps. 48).

D. On the third day they did sing, God stands in the congregation of God, he is
    a judge among the gods (Ps. 82).

E. On the fourth day they did sing, O Lord God to whom vengeance belongs, thou
    God to whom vengeance belongs, show yourself (Ps. 94).

F. On the fifth day they did sing, Sing we happily to God our strength, make a
    joyful noise to the God of Jacob (Ps. 81).

G. On the sixth day they did sing, The Lord is king and has put on glorious
    apparel (Ps. 93).

H. On the Sabbath-day they did sing, A Psalm, A song for the Sabbath-day (Ps.
    92)--

I. A psalm, a song for the world that is to come, for the day which is wholly
    Sabbath-rest for eternity.

M. 7:4